SCHOLASTIC

Month-by-Month
PRESCHOOL ALMANAC

Hundreds of Learning Activities
Just Right for Young Children

September October November December

January February March April

May June July August

by Annie Stiefel

NEW YORK • TORONTO • LONDON • AUCKLAND • SYDNEY
MEXICO CITY • NEW DELHI • HONG KONG • BUENOS AIRES

Teaching *Resources*

To Zach and Zoë

I want to thank all the children and parents I had the privilege of knowing, teaching, and learning from over the years at Little Bear Child Care.

Special appreciation to my friend and editor, Beth Button, for her meticulous attention while combing through my 27 original issues of The Preschool Almanac newsletter. Beth's diligent assistance helped shape the Month-by-Month Preschool Almanac into its book format.

Thanks also to Joyce Gerber, friend and teacher extraordinaire. Her contagious enthusiasm and dedication to children persuaded me long ago to continue my education.

My heartfelt thanks to Debby Sigovich, friend, mentor, and lover of books, for her caring input during my early years working with young children, and her invaluable help with the Almanac's book list.

Finally, special thanks to my mom, Jean Stiefel, for all her support and the many hours she spent illustrating the original newsletter. Heartfelt thanks always to my two children Zach and Zoë, and to their dad, Mark Eisenberg. Without the four of them, this book would not be.

Activities on pages 33 and 189 are adapted from *Fresh & Fun: October* by Deborah Rovin-Murphy and Frank Murphy (Scholastic, 2000) and *Read, Snack & Learn With Favorite Picture Books* by Jodi Simpson (Scholastic, 2004).

Cover design by Maria Lilja
Cover illustration by Jane Yamada
Interior design by Holly Grundon
Interior illustration by Milk 'n' Cookies

ISBN: 0-439-53152-7
Copyright © 2004 by Annie Stiefel.
Published by Scholastic Inc.
All rights reserved.
Printed in the U.S.A.

1 2 3 4 5 6 7 8 9 10 40 11 10 09 08 07 06 05 04

Contents

March

April

May

June

July

August

Welcome!

Welcome to the *Month-by-Month Preschool Almanac*! Just like the almanacs of old, this book is a touchstone—a useful source of information and an invaluable planning tool. It is filled with ideas, instruction, and guidance for those who fill their classrooms, homes, and hearts with young children. Whether you are a preschool teacher, a home daycare provider, an au pair, a parent, or a grandparent, the Preschool Almanac will help you provide a consistently rich, varied, and stimulating environment for the children in your care—all year long!

Meeting the Standards

The activities in this book align with the guidelines and recommended teaching practices set out by The National Association for the Education of Young Children and the International Reading Association (1998):

Recommended teaching practices:

* share books with children and model reading behaviors
* talk about letters by name and sounds
* establish a literacy-rich environment
* reread favorite stories
* engage children in language games
* promote literacy-related play activities
* encourage children to experiment with writing

Young children need developmentally appropriate experiences and teaching to support literacy learning. To this end, teachers can provide:

* positive, nurturing relationships with adults who engage in responsive conversations with children, model reading and writing behavior, and foster children's interest in and enjoyment of reading and writing;

* print-rich environments that provide opportunities and tools for children to see and use written language for a variety of purposes, with teachers drawing children's attention to specific letters and words;

* adults' daily reading of high-quality books to individuals or small groups, including books that positively reflect children's identity, home language, and culture;

* opportunities for children to talk about what is read and to focus on the sounds and parts of language as well as the meaning;

* teaching strategies and experiences that develop phonemic awareness, such as songs, fingerplays, games, poems, and stories in which phonemic patterns such as rhyme and alliteration are salient;

* opportunities to engage in play that incorporates literacy tools, such as writing grocery lists in dramatic play, making signs in block building, and using icons and words in exploring a computer game; and

* firsthand experiences that expand children's vocabulary, such as trips in the community and exposure to various tools, objects, and materials.

Source: Learning to Read and Write: Developmentally Appropriate Practices for Young Children © 1998 by The National Association for the Education of Young Children.

What's Inside

This book is a compilation of tried and tested ideas and activities from *The Preschool Almanac Newsletter*, a monthly publication I started after my sixth year as a home-based childcare provider. Although my patience, creativity, and energy served me well when I first began working with children, I saw that they seemed to learn best within a structure that linked their learning activities together. As I filled our days with enriching activities, art, books, and music, I began to develop a theme-based curriculum.

The *Almanac* is arranged into 12 monthly units, each with four themes (one per week). Every month, you'll find a wide variety of ideas to choose from: art projects, science and nature explorations, reading and math activities, creative movement, outdoor play, feltboard storytelling, songs, fingerplays, recipes, book lists, and much more. All of the activities and projects use easy-to-find materials—including many recycled items from your classroom or home—to help you create inexpensive, yet enriching, learning experiences.

The themes and corresponding activities in this book can be tailored to meet your particular needs. For instance, if your program does not meet every day, you may choose to extend one theme over several weeks. Or, if you already have a well-developed thematic curriculum in place, you might choose one or two new themes to add to your schedule. Perhaps you are looking for a great recipe or some new book ideas to complement your existing curriculum, or simply for a fresh activity on a rainy day. The *Almanac* puts countless activities and ideas right at your fingertips!

Benefits of a Theme-Based Curriculum

While you can pick and choose activities, songs, and fingerplays from the *Month-by-Month Preschool Almanac* at random, there are many advantages to following a structured, theme-based curriculum. For example, if you and your group make apple butter, children will certainly enjoy the experience. But if you do the same activity in the context of a week-long exploration of apples, you give children a foundation and a framework for that experience.

There are several more advantages to following a theme-based curriculum:

✳ You'll find that your days flow more smoothly and purposefully. Since preschoolers feel more secure and function best when there is a routine to their days, a structured curriculum can help improve classroom dynamics.

✳ Planning a structured curriculum and providing families with a schedule can increase family-initiated involvement. When I provide the families in my program with a copy of my weekly curriculum, I often get some nice surprises! For instance, on the morning of apple-tasting day, a mother and child arrived with a basket of assorted apples—including several varieties I didn't have. Not only was the child immensely proud to have helped pick out the apples, but there were enough to send several home with each child.

A Final Note

Although planning a curriculum for the year will help you to stay organized and focused, don't forget that spontaneity is important! I've often seen the benefits of seizing upon "teachable moments" in my own program. For instance, during our "Kings, Queens & Castles" week, workers arrived to take down two trees in our yard—on the morning we were planning to make shining armor and crowns. The children were in awe of the chainsaws and the men and women in hard hats, and I couldn't pass up the chance for an up-close and personal peek into a tree-trimmer's work. I also thought it would be a good opportunity to learn about the ages and stages of trees. So we asked the workers questions, took pictures, smelled the fresh-cut wood, played in the sawdust, counted tree rings, and put off making armor and crowns until after lunch. The children not only learned a great deal, but were also able to explore their curiosity about the world around them—an essential element of lifelong learning.

The *Month-by-Month Preschool Almanac* is a flexible tool, and there are many different ways to use it. However you choose to use this book, it will provide you with a valuable resource to keep you focused, motivated, and filled with a spirit of adventure. And this, in turn, will help the inquisitive young minds in your care to blossom and grow.

Enjoy!

Annie Stiefel

A Note About Safety

The projects in this book use materials that are safe for children to handle. However, adult supervision and guidance are necessary. Directions for several activities include special safety notes, for example, reminding you to keep children at a safe distance as you use a glue gun or cook on a stovetop. In addition, when cooking with children, check for food allergies first, especially for many of the recipes requiring nuts. Wash and dry all fruit and vegetables in advance, keep all perishables refrigerated before preparation, and have children wash and dry their hands before and after any cooking activity.

Look, Listen & Feel

If you're beginning the school year in September, it's is a good time to think about your philosophy for classroom management. Just as you introduce children to classroom routines and rules at the beginning of the year, you also decide your own role. Of course, your first concern is keeping children away from harm. Making their daily environment age-appropriate and as safe as possible is undoubtedly of utmost importance. But another role you play is to teach children social skills and productive ways to show their emotions. When children feel safe and secure in their surroundings, this is a much easier process. But how do you decide when to intervene and when to stand back?

Learning to give children time to work out their problems independently can be challenging. I have found that adopting the philosophy of "Look, Listen & Feel" can be very helpful when dealing with conflict.

Look

Unless there is immediate danger, it can be useful to give yourself enough time to observe the situation. After assessing what's causing trouble, try to share your observations with children in one objective sentence, such as *I see two friends who are angry with each other.*

Listen

When you take on the role of listener, you help children learn to solve problems on their own. Take time to stop what you're doing and give children your full attention. If children are trying to talk at the same time, help them slow down. Let each child speak, uninterrupted. Once children have had a chance to have their feelings heard, you can help them by acknowledge these feelings verbally: *Caroline, you're angry because Ashley won't give you your turn. Ashley, you're afraid Caroline won't give the dolls back.* You may be surprised to find that once their feelings are aired, children often come up with their own solutions.

When working with toddlers who can't yet express themselves verbally, it can help to provide labels for them: *Caroline, are you very angry right now?* You might then offer a few solutions and let them choose. For instance, *Would you both like to dress the dolls before we put them away? Or would you like to play in the sprinkler while the dolls have a rest?*

Feel

It's important to let children know that their feelings are accepted. Help children to recognize their own feelings by modeling empathic behavior, and by labeling emotions for them throughout the day, for example: *You seem a little sad* or *You seem very frustrated right now!* By doing this consistently, you will help children develop awareness of their emotions, understand them, and connect their feelings with language.

Implementing the "Look, Listen & Feel" approach can help guide children toward solving problems on their own. You may find that you'll need to intervene less as children learn new strategies for dealing with conflict. Using "Look, Listen & Feel" helps children become capable, independent, and caring people in the classroom environment and beyond.

Buses All Around

September is here, school is open, and big yellow school buses are back in action! While many children are fascinated by these great "dinosaurs of the road," some youngsters may be unfamiliar with them. These activities will help children learn all about school buses—an especially important topic for four-year-olds, since next year they may be riding the bus themselves!

Bring a Bus

Ask if anyone has toy buses at home, and invite them to bring them in to share with the group. Set them all out and ask, *How do the buses look the same? How are they different? What are some other ways that children might travel to school? Why do you think school buses are usually yellow?* (the color is easy to see, so that the vehicle can stay safe). *Do any of these buses have words on them? What do they say?*

Safety First!

Discuss bus rules:

* ❋ Stay sitting down.
* ❋ Talk quietly so that the driver can concentrate.
* ❋ Keep your hands and arms inside the bus.
* ❋ Do not eat or drink on the bus.
* ❋ Stand far away from the road while waiting for the bus.

Storytime

Share *This Is the Way We Go to School* by Edith Baer (Scholastic, 1990). This is a great multicultural, rhyming story that tells how children from around the world travel to school each day. After reading, invite children to build their own town with blocks, plastic figures, toy buses, and so on. Then have children use their pretend town to demonstrate how they get to school each day.

Backyard Bus

Preschoolers can't seem to wait for the day they can climb aboard the big yellow bus with their older siblings or neighbors! Give children a chance to not only to "ride" a bus, but to "drive" one as well.

You will need:

* refrigerator box (available at appliance stores)
* duct tape
* 4 large tuna cans (unopened)
* paper towel tube or wooden paint stirrer
* yellow, red, black, and blue paint and brushes
* cutting knife
* glue gun

(**SAFETY NOTE:** Steps involving knife or hot glue should be done by an adult, with children at a safe distance.)

1. Leave the bottom of the box shut and use duct tape to seal the top of the box. With a box cutter, cut out pieces to make the front windshield, the back window, a set of swinging doors, and windows along both sides. Then have children paint the bus yellow! Let dry.

2. Remove labels from tuna cans and, using hot glue, attach cans to the front and back of the bus for headlights. Then create a stop sign and two license plates from the cardboard you already cut out and have children paint them. They might also paint a name for their bus on the side. Attach the stop sign to a paper towel tube or wooden paint stirrer for children to role play with when the bus is finished. Glue license plate to bus.

3. Paint on "wheels" and place small chairs in the bus. Watch children drive away into the land of their imagination!

Hop on the Bus!

Bring dress-up clothes, backpacks, and lunchboxes out to your backyard bus for hours of role-playing fun. Let children take turns sitting on the bus and playing the roles of bus driver and crossing guard. Provide a stop sign for the crossing guard, and a special hat for the driver. Have some special badges or vests on hand for children to play crossing guard or safety officer.

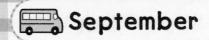

Fingerpaint Fun

First, discuss different kinds of buses. *What other kinds of buses are there besides school buses? Are all buses yellow? What other color might a bus be?*

Cut out a giant bus shape from butcher paper. Then, make a batch of fingerpaint together and let children fingerpaint their big bus! Have children start with yellow, and then add red or blue. Ask, *What color have you made by mixing yellow and red? What happens when you mix yellow and blue?*

* ❋ 1/2 cup white flour
* ❋ 2 cups water
* ❋ 1 tablespoon glycerin (available in drugstores)
* ❋ food coloring or powdered tempera in primary colors

1. Mix flour and 1/2 cup water in a saucepan over low heat until smooth.

2. Add remaining water and cook over medium heat until thick, stirring constantly for five minutes. Cool.

3. Add glycerin and food coloring or tempera and stir (divide into separate containers before adding coloring). Makes 1 1/2 cups.

Book Nook

The backyard bus (see page 12) can be a cozy place for storytelling!

Bus Stops by Taro Gomi (Chronicle, 1999)

Gus the Bus by Olga Cossi (Scholastic, 1989)

Maisy Drives the Bus by Lucy Cousins (Candlewick, 2000)

School Bus by Donald Crews (Greenwillow, 1993)

The Seals on the Bus by Lenny Hort (Holt, 2000)

The Wheels on the Bus by Maryann Kovalski (Little Brown, 1987)

Bus Full of Friends

Cut a large rectangle for each child from lightweight cardboard. Pour different colors of tempera paint onto paper plates. Have children "drive" small toy plastic vehicles through the paint and then onto the cardboard buses! Once dry, use permanent marker to draw rectangles and squares (for doors and windows) on the buses.

Have children bring in photos of themselves, family members, and friends. (Children can also use pictures of people cut from old magazines.) Let each child glue his or her photo onto the door of the bus and then arrange pictures of friends or family in the windows. Help them glue on recyclable plastic lids (such as yogurt tops) for wheels.

Apples, Apples, Apples

September's always a great time to learn about apples. If you have an apple orchard nearby, take children apple picking. Many orchards even have small trees that are perfect for preschoolers. But apples from the supermarket will work just as well!

All About Apples

Share a variety of apples: red, yellow, and green, small and large, speckled and striated, bumpy and smooth. Then try one or more of the following investigations.

✳ Fill a clear bowl with water and ask: *Will an apple sink or float?* Record children's predictions and then try it and see. (Apples float because about 25% of their volume is air.) Then, ask: *What happens to the water on the skin of the apple when you take the apple out of the water?* (It beads up and rolls off, especially if the apple has been waxed to make it shiny.)

✳ Encourage children to look at the bottom of the apple to see and feel the fuzzy, dried-up remains of the flower.

✳ Before cutting the apples, talk about their colors, sizes, smells, textures, and shapes. Compare the apples to other fruits, such as grapefruit and cherries. Then cut an apple open. Help children identify the pulp, the skin, and the core. The little pockets that hold the seeds are called carpels. Before you dig out the seeds, let children guess how many there are, then count them. Cut open another apple and see if it has the same number of seeds.

✳ Have a taste test! Invite children to taste several varieties of apples. Ask: *How are they different? Is one sweeter or more sour than the others? Are some softer or crisper than others? Which one do you like best?* Have children vote for their favorite, then record responses on a chart.

Apples Are for Eating

One of the best ways to use apples in the classroom is, of course, to eat them! See pages 16–17 for healthy recipes that make delicious use of the apple harvest. Let children help prepare the apples for cooking. Even very young children can cut an apple into small pieces with a plastic knife if the apple has been cored and quartered first.

Apple Chants & Fingerplays

Try these rhymes:

Apple Tree

Way up high in an apple tree,
*(form circles with index
fingers and thumbs, hold
arms up, and sway)*

Ten red apples smiled at me.
*(open hands to show ten
fingers and smile)*

I shook that tree
as hard as I could,
(clasp hands and shake)

Down they came,
*(hold arms up and then
sweep them downward)*

One, two, three, four, five,
six, seven, eight, nine, ten—

Mmm, were they good!
(rub tummy)

—Annie Stiefel

Who Eats Apples?

Who eats apples like we do?
Beavers, bears, and mice,
To name just a few.

Who loves apples like we do?
Beavers, bears, and mice,
Oh yes they do!

—Annie Stiefel

Apple T-Shirts

These t-shirts are perfect to wear on an apple-picking trip . . . or right in the classroom!

Have each child bring in a plain white t-shirt. Lay shirts flat and insert a piece of cardboard inside each. Then make "paint pads" by placing three large, clean, damp sponges in styrofoam trays. Spread a different color fabric paint (red, yellow, and green) on each sponge and pat off the excess onto the styrofoam.

Cut several apples in half, some vertically and some horizontally. Stick a fork into the skin of each apple to create a handle. Then show children how to press the apple onto the paint pad and stamp it onto the t-shirt. Allow paint to dry, then iron the shirts to set the paint before washing and wearing!

An Apple a Day

Teach children the saying "an apple a day keeps the doctor away!" Apples supply us with vitamins A and C, potassium, and fiber—so maybe it's true! Explain that healthy food helps us grow. Ask, *How do you think the apple gets what it needs to grow?* (The stem helps carry nutrients from the tree to the apple.)

Recipe

Easy Apple Butter

Enjoy this sweet spread on toast, biscuits, muffins, and peanut butter sandwiches. It is also delicious served warm over vanilla ice cream!

✳ 8 baking apples (peeled, cored, and cut into chunks)

✳ 1/4 teaspoon nutmeg

✳ 1/4 teaspoon ground cloves

✳ 1 teaspoon cinnamon

✳ 1/2 cup dark brown sugar

✳ juice of one lemon

1. Mix all ingredients together in a nine-inch square glass or ceramic casserole. Bake uncovered at 300°F for one hour.

2. Remove mixture and have an adult puree the mixture in a food processor or blender. Pour back into casserole and bake uncovered two more hours, stirring well after each hour.

3. Let cool. Makes 1 1/2 cups.

Note: You can easily double or triple this recipe as long as you have a very large, flat casserole in which to bake it.

Book Nook

Here are some great books to read while apple munching!

Applebet by Clyde Watson (Farrar Straus & Giroux, 1982)

Apples and Pumpkins by Anne Rockwell (Aladdin, 1994)

The Apple Tree by Zoe Hall (Scholastic, 1996)

How Do Apples Grow? by Betsy Maestro (HarperCollins, 2000)

Johnny Appleseed by Stephen Vincent Benet (McElderry, 2001)

Picking Apples and Pumpkins by Amy Hutchings (Cartwheel, 1994)

Ten Red Apples by Pat Hutchins (Greenwillow, 2000)

Apple Wreaths   **These apple wreaths will last indefinitely!**

1. Use large apples (two per child) with a dark red skin, such as Delicious. Cut the apples horizontally into 1/8-inch slices to reveal the star shape inside. (One large apple will yield approximately 10 slices.)

2. Soak the slices for five minutes in a solution of two cups water, 1/3 cup bottled lemon juice, and two tablespoons salt. Drain well and place in a single layer on a paper towel. Air dry for five to six days near a sunny window. Let children sample

the dried apple. Ask: *Which do you like better, fresh apples or dried? Where did the moisture go?*

3. To create a wreath, each child will need a six-inch cardboard wreath. Have children overlap the apple slices to cover one side of the wreath, and attach them with Tacky glue (available at craft stores). Once the glue is dry, let children sprinkle their wreaths with cinnamon. Decorate with cloves, cinnamon sticks, and ribbon.

Recipe

Rosie's Applesauce

The apple skins turn this applesauce a rosy color! The recipe got its name from the children in my group, who made up a story about a girl named Rosie who had pink cheeks from picking lots of apples outdoors. I'm not sure which children enjoy more, eating the applesauce or elaborating on the story each time we make it!

* 3 1/2 pounds apples, cored and quartered
* 1 3/4 cups water
* 1 tablespoon lemon juice
* 1/2 cup brown sugar
* 1 tablespoon cinnamon
* 1/2 teaspoon nutmeg
* 1/8 teaspoon ginger

1. Place apples, water, and lemon juice in a large saucepan. Bring to a boil over medium high heat, and then reduce to a simmer. (Supervise children closely for safety.) Cook uncovered until the apples are very soft, approximately 45 minutes.

2. Stir brown sugar, cinnamon, nutmeg, and ginger into the apple mixture and remove from heat. At this point, the room will smell delicious! Let cool. Then let children take turns mashing apples with potato masher. Serve warm or chilled. Makes two quarts.

Grow an Apple Plant

What would happen if you put soil and an apple seed in a little cup and kept it watered? Try it and see! First, put the seeds in the freezer for six weeks to let them stratify, a process which simulates winter. Then plant them in paper cups (one seed per cup) filled with moist soil. You'll see sprouts!

Apple Toss

Make some fun and inexpensive bean bags and help children develop gross motor skills. A sewing machine (or a volunteer with one!) makes this easier.

1. Collect used or new red, green, and yellow socks (or tights) in any size (yard sales and thrift shops are good sources). Each sock will yield three to four beanbags.

2. Fill the toe with a half-cup of dried beans or rice. Then use several safety pins to pin the sock closed next to the beans. Stitch four seams across the width of the sock. Cut between the seams as shown to create one beanbag. Then fill the sock again with another half-cup of beans. Stitch four more seams. Repeat until the sock is used up.

3. When the beanbags are finished, gather several baskets of different sizes and tie them together. Then let children stand back and toss their apples!

Kings, Queens & Castles

Children love stories about knights in shining armor, enchanted kingdoms, brave princesses, and ferocious, fire-breathing dragons. Storytime is even more magical when children join in the fantasy and become court jesters, dragons, kings, or queens. Bring the days of yore to life in your classroom!

Make a Castle

It's easy to turn an empty refrigerator box into an inexpensive and durable castle.

Ask a local appliance store for a refrigerator box. Leave the bottom of the box closed for stability, and open the top. The bottom of the box will be the floor of your castle! With a box cutter (with children at a distance), cut out windows, turrets, and a drawbridge (see illustration above). Then cut a hole in the drawbridge and attach a piece of rope, knotting it at one end. Cut a hole in the box just above the drawbridge, thread the other end of the rope through the hole, and knot it. Show children how to pull the rope tight when they want to raise the drawbridge! Let children decorate their castle. Add dress-up clothes, scarves, plastic crowns, and so on for a royal dramatic play center!

Super Scepters

For each scepter, you will need one paper towel tube. Help children stuff a ball of brightly colored paper, such as tissue paper or gift wrap, into the top of the tube. Then let children color their scepters with paint and markers. They can also add foil, rick-rack, bits of tissue paper, sequins, stickers, and glitter. Let children put on their armor and crowns (see page 20) and hold their scepters as they march in a fantasy parade! Explain that scepters represented the power of royalty.

A Dragon Visit

Create a dragon that children can "ride"!

1. Begin by removing the top and bottom from a large corrugated cardboard box. Staple a shoebox to the front of the box for the dragon's head.

2. Next, create shoulder straps by cutting two pieces of string or ribbon long enough to criss-cross over children's shoulders. Punch holes in the box and tie the straps on.

3. Finally, attach a long tail made from scrap cardboard or crepe paper to the back of the box. You can even make your dragon breathe fire by gluing some red, orange, and yellow crepe paper flames to the mouth!

4. Have children paint the dragon. When dry, they can create eyes, a nose, ears, and teeth with markers, paint, or construction paper cutouts.

5. Children can take turns "riding" the dragon by stepping in, pulling the box up to their waists, and sliding the straps over their shoulders.

Knights & Dragons

Share these fun facts and questions with children.

✳ A knight's job was to fight for his king and queen. He wore heavy armor and a helmet covering his face.

✳ Knights had a special design called "a coat of arms" painted on their shields to help identify them in battle. *If you were a knight, what would your coat of arms look like?*

✳ Dragons are imaginary magical lizards, larger than elephants. They are often described as having long fangs, twin horns, bat-like wings, scales, and the ability to breathe fire!

✳ Red, green, black, and gold are common dragon colors.

✳ Ask: *Were knights and princesses real? Were kings and queens real? What about dragons?*

Shining Armor & Crowns

Children can create miniature suits of armor and sparkling crowns to add to their dramatic play!

To make **armor**, cut two 8- by 12-inch pieces of cardboard for each child. Then punch a hole in the corners of each "plate of armor." Connect the front and back plates with four pieces of ribbon or string. Thread ribbon or string through the holes and knot at each end to secure, forming waist and shoulder straps. Let children decorate their armor with silver and gold contact paper, paint, glitter, and stickers. Children can put on the armor by sliding it over their heads.

To make **crowns**, cut a wide strip of colored construction paper or lightweight cardboard for each child. Cut the top edge of the strip in a zig-zag pattern. Then let children decorate their strips with gold and silver contact paper, foil, paint, stickers, glitter, sequins, and beads. When dry, wrap around children's heads and secure the ends with tape.

Let children put on their crowns and settle in for a good book.

Everyone Knows What a Dragon Looks Like by Jay Williams (Simon & Schuster, 1976)

The Good Stepmother by Marguerita Rudolf (Simon & Schuster, 1992)

The Knight and the Dragon by Tomie dePaola (Putnam, 1980)

A Medieval Feast by Aliki (HarperCollins, 1983)

The Paper Bag Princess by Robert Munsch (Annick, 1985)

Princess Smartypants by Babette Cole (Putnam, 1987)

Sir Cedric by Roy Gerrard (Farrar Straus & Giroux, 1984)

King & Queen for a Day

Let children take turns being king or queen for a day. Decorate a chair with crepe paper streamers and a soft cushion to serve as a throne. The king or queen can wear a crown, hold a scepter, or even put on a cape! Ask the royal highness to choose the day's snack or lunch, lead the line, pick a storybook, or head up a game of Follow the Leader.

Fabulous Fall

This month, children might begin to notice the change in the seasons: the weather is cooler, and depending on where you live, sweaters and jackets come out of the closet again. The leaves on the trees may be changing color, and school buses are on the roads once more. Young children love to collect and sort, and this is the perfect season for it. Autumn's bounty will provide plenty of treasures for youngsters. Take a walk and look for signs of autumn with children. Encourage them to gather leaves, nuts, seeds, and pods!

Tree People

Transform your group into a colorful forest!

One at a time, have children lie down on a long roll of butcher paper. Trace around each child (so that it will look like a row of children when you are finished), then tape the paper to a wall. Supply children with tempera paints (in red, orange, yellow, green, and brown) and a variety of sponges, and let them sponge paint their tracings and write their names. Once dry, let children glue on real leaves for hands, feet, and hair!

Leaves, Leaves, Leaves

Go on an autumn walk and collect fallen leaves and dried grasses. As children collect leaves, ask: *What color is this leaf? How many points does it have? Does it have a scent? Can you find another one like it?* (Also encourage children to look for acorns, pinecones, and seedpods.) Once indoors, there's lots you can do with your autumn treasures:

✳ Fill your water or sand table with leaves to sort by color, size, and shape.

✳ Make leaf rubbings with crayon.

✳ Use acorns and leaves as math manipulatives.

✳ Put a basket of leaves and other fall finds in the dramatic play center.

Ratatouille

Ratatouille (rah-tah-TOO-ee) is fun to say and delicious to eat! It's also a healthy, hearty way to enjoy the fall vegetable crop.

When making this seasonal dish, you'll need plenty of little helping hands! Children (using plastic knives) can easily dice eggplant, zucchini, peppers, and yellow squash. Let children sample the veggies raw, and again when cooked. Ratatouille can be served warm over pasta, over rice, or on pita or French bread to make a pizza. Or try it cold with cannelloni beans tossed in.

* 1/2 cup olive oil
* 2 medium onions, chopped (2 cups)
* 6 cloves garlic
* 4 ripe tomatoes, chopped (5 cups)
* 2 medium zucchini, cubed
* 2 medium yellow squash, cubed
* 1 large eggplant, peeled and cut into 1/2-inch cubes
* 1 large red pepper, diced
* 1 large green pepper, diced
* 1 pound mushrooms, quartered (optional)
* 1 cup tomato sauce
* 1 tablespoon dried oregano
* 1 pound mozzarella, cubed
* salt and pepper to taste

1. Saute garlic and onions in oil in a large pot on low heat for 10 minutes until the onions are translucent. (Supervise children closely for safety.)

2. Add vegetables, tomato sauce, and oregano. Cover and simmer about 25 minutes, stirring occasionally. The vegetables should be tender, but not mushy.

3. Uncover and remove from heat for 15 minutes.

4. Stir in cheese and add salt and pepper to taste. Makes 14 cups.

Fabulous Foliage

Put children on Leaf Lookout! Who will spot the first leaf to turn color outside?

When color is at its peak, bring easels and smocks outside. Supply children with large sheets of white paper cut into leaf shapes, and red, yellow, orange, and brown paints. Then encourage children to paint the colors they see.

Nut, Nut, Squirrel

Try this fun variation on Duck, Duck, Goose.

Have children sit in a circle and choose one child to be the "squirrel." The squirrel walks around the circle, tapping each child (gently!) on the head with a nut or acorn, saying the word "nut" each time. At any point, the squirrel taps a child, says "squirrel," and drops the nut or acorn into the child's lap. That child (who is then the new squirrel) picks up the nut and chases the old squirrel around the circle and back to his or her seat. Continue play until each child has had a chance to be the squirrel.

Leaf Art

There's a lot you can do with leaves! Try some of these easy art activities:

✳ Make leaf prints. Lightly paint the top sides of leaves with red, orange, or yellow paint. Gently press onto paper.

✳ Cut large leaf shapes from construction paper and use an eyedropper to drop on red, orange, green, and brown tempera. Have children fold their leaves in half and press down. Open for a symmetrical autumn surprise.

✳ Gather leaves and let dry. Invite children to crumble them to make "leaf glitter." Use in the art center as you would glitter.

✳ Use two pieces of contact paper to sandwich leaves and scraps of colored tissue paper. Display in the window and let the fall sun shine in!

✳ Have children make their own leaves by tracing their hands onto colored construction paper. Staple several sheets of brown construction paper to a bulletin board to make a "trunk" and staple children's "leaves" to the top.

Autumn Song

Come, Little Leaves
(to the tune of "Hush Little Baby")

"Come little leaves," said the wind one day. *(beckon with hands)*

Come to the meadow with me and play. *(sway back and forth)*

Put on your colors of red and gold, *(hold one hand up on red and the other hand up on gold)*

Summer is done and the days grow cold! *(hug body and shiver)*

—Annie Stiefel

Recipe

Z Cookies

Z is for zucchini, of course! These cookies are soft, moist, and delicious. If you triple the recipe, you will use up one whole pound of this yummy fall squash! If you have leftovers, Z cookies also freeze well.

* 1 stick butter, softened
* 1 cup sugar
* 1 egg
* 1/4 teaspoon ground cloves
* 1/2 teaspoon salt
* 1 teaspoon cinnamon
* 1 teaspoon baking powder
* 2 cups flour
* 1/2 cup raisins
* 1/2 cup sunflower seeds
* 1 cup grated zucchini

1. Cream together butter and sugar. Mix in egg.

2. Mix together cloves, salt, cinnamon, baking powder, and flour. Add to the butter, sugar, and egg mixture. Stir.

3. Stir in raisins, sunflower seeds, and zucchini.

4. Drop by tablespoons onto greased cookie sheets. Bake at 375°F about 12 minutes, until tops and bottoms are barely browned. Makes 30 cookies.

Book Nook

Fall in love with a good book! Here are some great autumn stories.

Autumn Leaves by Ken Robbins (Scholastic, 1998)

Every Autumn Comes the Bear by Jim Arnosky (Putnam, 1996)

Fall Leaves Fall by Zoe Hall (Scholastic, 2000)

Marmalade's Yellow Leaf by Cindy Wheeler (Harper & Row, 1982)

Nuts to You by Lois Ehlert (Harcourt, 1993)

Red Leaf, Yellow Leaf by Lois Ehlert (Harcourt, 1991)

School by Emily Arnold McCully (Harper & Row, 1987)

When Autumn Comes by Robert Maass (Holt, 1990)

Relax!

Sometimes life can move all too quickly. Technology, media, and packed schedules all seem to make our world move faster and faster—and it can be difficult to keep up! Taking the time to relax and get back to basics is important for adults and children alike. Of course, exercise, laughter, daily routines, hugs, and nurturing help children feel balanced. But it's never too early to teach children to stop, relax, and listen to their minds and bodies. September is a great time to start! Why not get down on the floor with children and introduce some yoga poses and simple breathing exercises as a tool for relaxation?

What's Yoga All About?

Yoga is an exercise system developed in India thousands of years ago to promote physical and mental health. Hatha Yoga, the study of physical discipline through the practice of asanas (or poses) and breathing, is a natural way for young children to release tension because they love to express themselves by moving their bodies. In addition to its calming effects, yoga can also be lots of fun for children: many of the poses are based on the movements and shapes of animals, which children love to imitate. In the process of learning the different postures, yoga also helps children to develop and improve concentration, muscle control, balance, and coordination. The poses also help to keep young spines and joints flexible as they grow.

I began practicing yoga when I was 10. I was intrigued by the different positions as well as their names: Halasan, the Plough; Bhujangasan, the Cobra; Chakrasana, the Wheel; and Kakasana, the Crow! I learned hundreds of asanas and their names over the next seven years, but more importantly, I developed an ability to concentrate, to watch, and to listen —not only to the instructor, but also to myself. I left each class feeling balanced, strengthened, and more sure of myself. It helped me tremendously throughout my adolescent years and has continued to be a resource throughout my life.

Yoga & Children

Yoga has been so important to me that I decided to incorporate it into my early childhood program. As adults, we teach children how to stay healthy through good diet, nutrition, and hygiene habits, but we can also teach them how to develop healthy responses to the challenges they will encounter in their lives. You can show children how to turn problems into opportunities by modeling effective problem-solving techniques and creative methods of dealing with the choices and changes that will come their way. I have found that yoga is a wonderful tool for this purpose.

You will find a selection of simple yoga poses on the following pages to get you started. Relax and enjoy!

Animal Action

Got cabin fever? If children seem restless, if you want to focus their attention, or if you need to help them transition from one activity to another, do some yoga! Get down the floor and show them how to stretch like cats, crow like roosters, and jump like frogs. This may produce a few giggles, but it will also leave children refreshed, calm, and ready to learn and play.

Yoga Tips

Yoga is best performed barefoot and on an empty stomach. A good time to do yoga is in the morning before snack, or as a prelude to more active play outside. Right after nap is also a great time for yoga, when children's bodies are relaxed.

Start every yoga session with a good stretch on tiptoes, fingers pointed to the sky. Finish with a relaxing exercise that children can do lying on their backs as they follow your directions: *Scrunch up every muscle in your face so it's very tight. Hold it and then relax. Take a big breath in and out. Then repeat with hands, arms, feet, and toes.*

Stretch Like a Dog

This pose, also called the Downward Dog, stretches and strengthens backs, hamstrings, and arms.

Begin by kneeling on all fours. Keeping your hands in place, push up on your toes and then roll your heels towards the floor, keeping your hips high up in the air and moving your head between the arms and towards the knees. Hold this position as long as it is comfortable and then come down. Lay on your back and relax. Then try it again!

Arch Like a Cat

Cats keep their bodies supple and limber by stretching every day!

Begin on all fours with your back level, like a table. Then slowly dip your chin down until it touches the floor. Next, in a smooth motion, tuck your chin into your chest and lift your back up into an arch as you pull your tummy in tight. Slowly release and relax your back until it's flat like a table again. Then sit back on your heels and say "meow"! This is a great stretch to do after a midday nap.

Roar Like a Lion

The Lion posture exercises all of the face muscles and gives arms and fingers a good stretch.

Sit on your heels and place your hands palms-down on your knees. Take a deep breath, open your eyes very wide, and roll your eyeballs up to the ceiling. At the same time, exhale with a very loud *haaaa* and stick your tongue out! Hold for a count of three. As you inhale, close your eyes and relax for a minute. Repeat a few times, then invite children to lean forward, stiffening their arms and opening their fingers wide on their knees as they do the Lion pose. This is a wonderful exercise when children are feeling cranky!

Work Like a Wood Chopper

Wood choppers have strong arms, strong backs and lots of energy! This posture is a great way to release tension or excess energy.

Stand with your legs apart and hands clasped together above your head. Then look up, dropping your head back, while you arch your spine and stretch your arms backwards. Tighten your buttock muscles as you do this to protect your lower back. Then bring your arms forward and down, letting them swing between your legs. Repeat, increasing the speed until everyone is warmed up and breathing quickly.

Jump Like a Frog

This posture improves balance while strengthening ankles, feet, and legs!

Squat on the floor. Start with your hands on the floor for balance, and then roll onto your toes. Practice shifting your weight from heels to toes several times, then put your hands on top of your head. Then try balancing on your toes again. When everyone is ready, start hopping and croaking! Toddlers who can't yet balance on their toes can hop flat-footed with their hands on their knees. To keep children from bumping into each other, invite them to pretend they are each on their own lilypad!

Crow Like a Rooster

Here's a fun way to get the energy going in the morning or after a nap. This gentle stretch introduces children to deep breathing, and also strengthens leg and back muscles.

Begin by standing straight with your hands at your sides. Close your eyes and listen to your breath move in and out of your body. Then open your eyes, and while taking in a slow, deep breath, raise your arms so that they are parallel to the ground. As you begin to exhale, sing *Cock-a-doodle-doo!*, then slowly lower your arms while exhaling the rest of your breath. Then close your eyes again and rest. Repeat three or four times. When children have mastered this technique, show them how to rise up onto their toes as they raise their arms, and come down onto their heels as they lower their arms.

Book Nook

Learn to help children exercise their bodies and minds with these great teaching resources.

Children's Book of Yoga by Thia Luby (Clear Light, 1998)

Like a Fish in Water: Yoga for Children by Isabelle Koch (Inner Traditions, 1999)

20-Minute Yoga Workouts by Alice Christensen (Fawcett, 1995)

Yoga for Children by Mary Stewart (Fireside, 1993)

Yoga Games for Children by Danielle Bersma & Marjoke Visscher (Hunter House, 2003)

Stand Like a Stork

A good source for stork photos is **www.nwoutdoorphoto. com/storks**

Show children a picture of a stork standing on one leg. Explain that this is how they sleep, resting one leg at a time!

Stand quietly with your hands at your sides. Bend one knee, raising your foot behind you. When you have your balance, put your palms together and raise them to chest height. As children follow your movements, ask: *Can you count slowly to three without losing your balance? How about 10?* When children have had a chance to practice holding the pose, invite them to try it with their eyes closed. This calming exercise helps develop concentration and balance.

Trikes & Bikes

Bikes come in all sizes and colors. Unicycles have one wheel, bicycles have two wheels, and tricycles have three. They are powered by our own energy and are used for fun, exercise, and transportation all over the world. Take time to set up a safe environment for bike riding so that children can practice this new challenge every day! (Make sure children wear bike helmets.)

Bicycle Safety

Together, make a list of bike safety rules, such as *stay out of the road, always watch where you're going, and only ride with a grown-up around.* Outdoors, set clearly marked riding space boundaries. Review the rules and safe areas each day before children hop on their bikes. Remember, even if children are only riding on the blacktop, it's never too early to teach the importance of wearing bike helmets every time they go for a ride. Ask families to provide a well-fitting helmet for children to use at school. The helmet should be worn low on the forehead and fastened snugly under the chin.

Bike Trail

Children love to follow a winding road with their trikes, bikes, or other riding toys.

Mark off a curvy trail on pavement with chalk, or by sprinkling thin lines of flour on grass. Use your trail for a game of Follow the Leader or even as an obstacle course. You can create a tunnel by cutting away the top and bottom of a large cardboard appliance box and laying it on its side. Make your own highway cones by spray-painting gallon-size milk jugs orange and filling them with sand. These are great for practicing turns, stops, and weaving in and out. You can also use them to mark off safe areas for trike riding.

Pedal to the Music

Bring a tape player and music outside along with trikes and riding toys. Have a selection of slow and fast music, classical and jazz, and children's favorite tunes. Challenge children to coordinate their pumping legs to the beat of the music! As children pedal, ask, *Do you feel your thigh and leg muscles working hard as you push the pedals?*

To add to the fun, give each rider a silly hat to wear. Or, have a few volunteers blow bubbles for the cyclists to ride through, or make a pile of leaves and invite children to pedal through them!

Bike Benefits

Bike riding is great for large motor skills, coordination, and balance. When done in a group, it can also improve listening and social skills, and give children practice in following directions. As children ride, they gather important information about direction, control, and the stop-and-go element of travel.

Wild Wheels

Explain that wheels help make things move. Can children explain why this is so? Why does a tricycle have three wheels, but a big truck has as many as 18?

Children can study circles and movement as they create their very own wheels.

Look at some different types of wheels, including those on a bike or trike. Explain that spokes are the rods coming from the center of a wheel that keep the wheel from wobbling as you ride.

Have children create their own wheels from paper or cardboard circles in various sizes. For spokes, they can glue on bits of plastic straws, string, yarn, ribbon, dry spaghetti or fettucini, pipe cleaners, twigs, or craft sticks. At the center of each, for the "hub," they can glue a button, coin, round hard candy, or a round paper scrap. Display on a bulletin board with a banner reading "We're on the Go!"

Fruit Wheels

Children can create their own set of wheels—with "spokes"!

1. Draw simple trike frames on construction paper, leaving out the wheels.

2. Then place paper towels or sponges on paper plates and pour a small amount of tempera paint onto each. Dab off the excess paint on the paper plate, so that the paper towel or sponge becomes an "inkpad."

3. Next, cut lemons, grapefruit, and oranges in half and insert a fork into the skin of each one to use as a handle. Invite children to create wheels by dipping the fruit into the paint and then onto their papers! You can also create miniature wheels with spools, corks, or milk caps.

Take these books out for a spin!

The Bear's Bicycle by Emilie Warren McLeod (Little Brown, 1986)

Bicycle Book by Gail Gibbons (Holiday House, 1995)

Bikes by Anne Rockwell (Dutton, 1987)

Curious George Rides a Bike by H.A. Rey (Houghton Mifflin, 1952)

Duck on a Bike by David Shannon (Blue Sky, 2002)

The Red Racer by Audrey Wood (Simon & Schuster, 1996)

Stella and Roy by Ashley Wolff (Dutton, 1993)

Safety License

Whether they're driving a toy car, a trike, or a bike, children enjoy carrying a grown-up "driver's license"!

1. Show children a real driver's license. Explain that they can create their own licenses to show that they know how to stay safe on the road. Take a photo of each child (or have family members bring one in from home) and trim the photo to "driver's license" size.

2. Next, help children glue their photo to the upper-right corner of a blank index card. Ask children to tell you their name, age, birthday, address, and hair and eye color. You can measure and record children's height as well. Print all the information on the card under the heading "Safety License" and let each child decorate the back of his or her license with stickers and stars.

3. Then laminate the card, punch a hole in the top, and loop yarn or ribbon through the hole. Children can wear their licenses around their necks as they drive and ride.

Fire Safety

As parents, caregivers, and teachers, it's important that we give children accurate information about fire safety. Since National Fire Prevention Week is in October, this is a great time to begin a fire safety program. It's also a perfect opportunity to visit your local fire station or invite a firefighter to visit the classroom. Many fire departments will bring a truck and equipment right to your school or center!

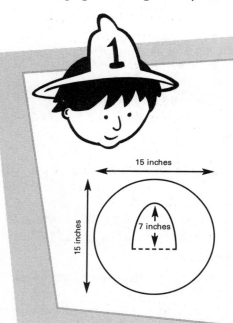

15 inches

15 inches

7 inches

Firefighter's Hat

For each child, cut out a 15-inch circle from red posterboard or lightweight cardboard that children have painted red. Cut out a seven-inch "U" shape and fold up the resulting flap.

Help children label their hats with their names and badge numbers. They can decorate the hats with stickers, or draw emblems from your local fire station.

Fire Drill

Practice fire drills with children regularly. Agree on a place outside where children, teachers, and family members would meet to wait for the fire department in the event of a fire. Let children hear the smoke alarm or warning bell so that they will recognize it as a signal to leave the building. Teach them to walk quickly (not run), and once outside, to stay out until an adult tells them it's okay to return.

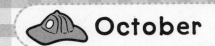

Crawl, Crawl, Crawl

Smoke can be just as dangerous as fire. Teach children how to exit a smoke-filled room by crawling low on their hands and knees, where the air will be cleaner.

You can make practicing this technique fun. Simply one side of a large sheet under the pillows of a couch, or attach it to the edge of a table or wall with masking tape. Hold the other side of the sheet and shake gently to create "smoke." Then let children crawl under the sheet and out the other side to safety. Review this procedure each month.

Stop, Drop & Roll

Another life-saving technique that young children can easily master is Stop, Drop, and Roll. Read the following directions aloud and invite children to act out each step.

If your clothes ever catch fire, this is how to put the fire out.

STOP: Stop where you are. Don't run!

DROP: Drop to the ground.

ROLL: Cover your face with your hands and roll over and over to put out the fire.

Turn Stop, Drop, and Roll into a chant and recite the rules frequently!

Put Out the Fire

Help develop motor control and teamwork as children form a firefighter's company!

Organize children into groups of four. They might like to wear their firefighters' hats for this activity (see page 32). Have each group stand in a row. Explain that both sand and water can put out fires and they will be putting out a pretend fire with sand! (You can also try this activity with water if it's warm outside!)

Each row needs two buckets, one filled with sand and the other empty. Place at opposite ends of the rows. Give the child standing next to the sand bucket a paper cup and invite him or her to fill the cup and pass it down the row. When it gets to the child next to the empty bucket, that child pours it into the bucket and passes the empty cup back down the row. Children continue until all sand has been moved. Congratulate each "company" on their teamwork!

Safe or Not Safe?

For this activity, you will need two empty tissue boxes. Cover one with green paper and label it Safe. Cover the other with red paper and label it Not Safe.

Draw or cut out magazine pictures of objects that keep people safe (such as a fire extinguisher, potholder, smoke detector, bike helmet, car seat, and so on) and objects that are unsafe (such as a book of matches, lighter, candle, sharp objects, and so on).

Show the pictures to children and talk about each item: what it is, how it is used, and why it is safe or dangerous. As a group, sort the pictures and place them in the correct boxes.

Book Nook

Start fire safety discussions with a good book.

Engine Shapes by Bruce McMillan (Lothrop, 1988)

Fighting Fires by Susan Kuklin (Bradbury, 1993)

Firefighters A to Z by Jean Johnson (Walker, 1985)

Fire Fighters by Norma Simon (Simon & Schuster, 1995)

"Fire! Fire!" Said Mrs. McGuire by Bill Martin, Jr. (Harcourt, 1996)

Fireman Small by Wong Herbert Yee (Houghton Mifflin, 1994)

Fire Truck by Peter Sís (Greenwillow, 1999)

No Dragons for Tea: Fire Safety for Kids by Jean Penziwol (Kids Can Press, 1999)

More Fire Safety Tips

You can bring fire safety awareness into your classroom throughout the year. Talk about fire safety rules when you cook with a stove, microwave, or toaster. Discuss fire prevention when lighting birthday candles, campfires, or barbecue grills (remind children that matches and lighters are tools for adults only—they often look like toys to children). Let children watch as you change smoke detector batteries, and explain how the device helps keep them safe.

Spooky & Kooky

Children delight in dress-up and fantasy play! This week, add hats, face paint, and a few brooms to the dramatic play area. Most preschoolers love Halloween, but some masks and costumes are frightening to young children. Help prepare them by letting them play with some "friendly" masks (such as a simple paper plate with eyes, nose, and mouth cut out). Reassure children that behind each mask they see on Halloween, there's a person just like them! To address any fears children might have, you can also ask, *Do real people have green faces? Who do you think is under that costume? What can we do when we're afraid?*

Pumpkin Fun

There's a lot you can do with this orange fruit!

* Put a teaspoon of vinegar, one cup water, and food coloring in a bowl. Add pumpkin seeds and stir, then spread on paper towel to dry. Use as math manipulatives or "painting" (draw with glue on paper, then sprinkle seeds on). It's great fine-motor practice!

* At circle time, blow up an orange balloon and use a black marker to draw eyes, nose, and mouth. Use your jack o' lantern to introduce any pumpkin activity.

I Saw a Little Ghost

Children can make their own ghost finger puppets.

Have each child drape a white tissue over his or her index finger. Wrap a piece of tape around the tissue (loosely, at the first joint of the child's finger) to form the head of the ghost. Then make two dots for eyes on each child's puppet with a black marker. Recite the following poem and invite children to act it out with their finger puppets. Preschoolers delight in making their ghost puppets jump on the word "BOO!"

I saw a little ghost,
(hold up ghost puppet, look surprised)

He saw me too.
(open eyes wide)

I said "Hi"
(wave with puppetless hand)

And he said, "BOO!"
(shout "BOO" and move finger puppet in jumping motion)

—Annie Stiefel

Ghosts & Spiders

Children use their hands and feet to create spooky creatures!

To make **ghosts**, pair children up and have partners trace each other's bare feet on heavy white paper. They cut out the shapes, lay the cut-outs with toes pointing down, and voila! Ghosts! Provide wiggle eyes, paper scraps, glitter, yarn, and glue for children to decorate their ghosts. Punch a hole in the top of each ghost, thread with string, and hang from the ceiling or windows.

To make **spiders**, have children place one hand (fingers spread) on a sheet of black paper. Trace the outline of the four fingers (do not include the thumb) using chalk or a white crayon. Then trace another hand. Cut out the spiders, glue together as shown, and punch holes for eyes. Let children decorate their spiders with glue and glitter, and hang from the ceiling and windows! You can even drape a bit of gauze over the spiders to make webs.

Orange Putty

Recipe

Children can bounce it, snap it, or stretch it!

This rubbery putty is made from ordinary glue and liquid starch. Playing with it will help children strengthen fine-motor skills!

* 1/2 cup white glue
* 2 drops yellow food coloring
* 1 drop red food coloring
* 1/4 cup liquid starch (use a new bottle of starch for best results)

Mix glue and food coloring together. Then add the starch slowly, stirring until glue begins to ball up and become rubbery. (If the putty becomes too stiff, add more glue. If it's too soft, add a bit more starch.) Store in an airtight container in refrigerator. Makes 1/2 cup.

Spooky, Kooky Pizza

Children will enjoy making this tasty, healthy recipe as they measure, pour, pat, and decorate the dough. This recipe makes eight mini-pizzas.

* 2 1/4 cups flour
* 1 1/4 sticks unsalted butter, cut into bits
* 3 tablespoons sugar
* 1/4 teaspoon salt
* 1/2 cup cold water
* 1 teaspoon vanilla

Toppings: sliced and chopped apples and pears, shredded coconut, and cinnamon sugar.

1. Combine flour, butter, sugar, and salt in a mixer until it is the consistency of coarse meal.

2. Add water and vanilla. Continue to mix until the ingredients just begin to clump together. (You may not need to use all the water.) Do not overmix.

3. Divide the dough into eight pieces and form each piece into a ball. Let children roll or pat out a five-inch diameter pizza with each piece.

4. Have children spread their pizzas with peanut butter, apple butter, a bit of jam, or any combination of these.

5. Have children decorate their pizzas with the toppings to create jack o' lantern faces.

6. Cook on ungreased cookie sheets at 400°F for 15 minutes, or until golden brown.

Paint a Pumpkin

Take a trip to a pick-your-own pumpkin patch (many offer hayrides and cider too). Back in the classroom, give children different colors of tempera paint, and colored contact paper cut into triangles, circles, squares, and rectangles. Help children peel off the backing and stick the shapes onto their pumpkins, creating faces or designs. Then have children paint their pumpkins (the entire surface). When paint is completely dry, children can peel off the shapes to reveal the bright orange skin underneath. Line up all the pumpkins for everyone to admire!

A Spider on My Head!

Be prepared for lots of giggles when children put on these silly headbands!

To begin, cut a two-inch wide strip of oaktag or heavy paper to make a headband for each child. Let children sponge-paint their headbands with tempera paint.

Next, cut eight strips of black construction paper for each child. Work with children to accordion-fold all the "spider legs" to make them springy.

Wrap the headbands around children's heads and tape in back to secure. Next, tape the spider legs to the headbands, four on each side. Children can wear their headbands as they do the "Halloween Hokey Pokey."

You put your scary face in,
You put your scary face out,
You put your scary face in,
And you shake it all about.
You say "Trick or Treat"
And you turn yourself around,
That's what it's all about!

The springy spider legs will jiggle with each step! Invite children to help make up new verses by replacing the words "scary face" with "funny feet," "long legs," "spider head," and so on.

Ghastly Ghostly Potato Prints

Children can make spooky stamps!

1. To make a set of four ghost stamps, cut two large potatoes in half. Carve a simple ghost shape (or use a ghost cookie cutter to press in lines) on the surface, and with a potato peeler, pare away everything around it to create a ghost shape. Using the sharp end of the peeler, dig out two eyes and a mouth.

2. Make a handle by inserting a fork into the skin of each potato half.

3. Place paper towels or sponges on paper plates and pour a small amount of white tempera paint onto each.

4. Dab off the excess paint on the paper plate, so that the paper towel or sponge becomes an "inkpad."

5. Have children press the ghost stamp into the "inkpad" and then press it onto black construction paper.

Owl Fun

Sing this fingerplay to the tune of "I'm a Little Teapot."

I saw a little owl,
(hold hands to eyes like binoculars)

High in a tree,
(raise hands over head)

I looked at him,
(put hands on hips)

And he looked at me.
(hold hands to eyes again)

When the moon came out,
(form a circle with arms)

The owl said,
"Whooooooo!"

He flapped his wings,
(flap arms)

And away he flew!

—Annie Stiefel

Book Nook

Picture books are a non-threatening way to explore the spooky images of Halloween.

Georgie by Robert Bright (Doubleday, 1959)

Georgie and the Noisy Ghost by Robert Bright (Doubleday, 1971)

Georgie's Halloween by Robert Bright (Doubleday, 1972)

It's Halloween! by Jack Prelutsky (Greenwillow, 1988)

The Little Old Lady Who Was Not Afraid of Anything by Linda Williams (Crowell, 1986)

Mouse's First Halloween by Lauren Thompson (Simon & Schuster, 2000)

On Halloween Night by Ferida Wolff (Mulberry, 1997)

Pumpkin Eye by Denise Fleming (Holt, 2001)

Scary, Scary Halloween by Eve Bunting (Clarion, 1988)

The Teeny Tiny Woman by Paul Galdone (Houghton Mifflin, 1984)

What a Scare, Jesse Bear by Nancy White Carlstrom (Simon & Schuster, 1999)

Handwashing 101

My first year as a childcare provider was exciting, but it also presented a unique challenge. As the year unfolded, I honed my skills working with preschoolers and their families—but I also caught more colds than I had caught in the previous ten years put together! When I told my doctor about the frequency with which I was catching colds, he advised me to wash my hands frequently throughout the day, and to keep my hands away from my face. I took his advice, and by the time cold season rolled around the following autumn, I was ready for it!

Start a Sink Sing-Along

Develop a repertoire of "sink songs" and poems to reinforce handwashing before snacks, meals, and cooking projects, and after using the bathroom. *This Is the Way We Wash Our Hands* (with substitute verses such as *get them wet*, *make a lather*, *rinse our hands*, and *dry them off*) keeps children scrubbing for the recommended 30 seconds.

You can also chant this poem with children, even when they aren't washing:

> This little hand is a good little hand,
> This little hand is its brother;
> Together they wash and they wash
>   and they wash—
> One hand washes the other.

Books can also add an element of fun to the topic of handwashing. Judith Rice's *Those Mean Nasty Dirty Downright Disgusting Invisible Germs* (Gryphon House, 1990) and Tony Ross's *Wash Your Hands* (Kane Miller, 2000) will quickly become favorites with children.

In addition to proper handwashing techniques, you can incorporate the theme of conservation by creating child-size paper towels: simply "saw" entire paper towel rolls in half with a serrated knife. You can also teach children to save water by turning off the tap while they lather up or brush their teeth.

You'll find, as I did that first year, that this diligence will pay off. Though children will always catch colds, germs won't spread as quickly—and everyone will stay healthier during the fall and winter. Perhaps someday a remedy for the common cold will be discovered. But until then . . . bring on the soap and keep on scrubbing!

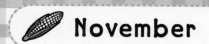

Autumn Corn

Corn has always been one of our country's food staples. It was the basis for the diet of Native Americans and the early settlers, who called it maize and ground it for bread, porridge, fried corncakes, and pudding. Today, we still use corn in margarine, syrup, cooking oil, bread, tortillas, pancakes, chowder, and more. Children love to explore, count, pop, and eat this mainstay of the American table.

Corncob Prints

Create a fall-patterned "tablecloth" for a special classroom meal.

Gather several ears of dried multi-colored corn. Discard any husks. Make paint pads by cutting pieces of felt or paper towel to fit the bottom of several large foam produce trays. Spread several tablespoons of tempera paint on each pad (one red, one yellow, one blue).

Let children roll the corncob on the paint pads and then onto a large piece of butcher paper.

Maize Madness

Making popcorn engages all the senses. Children love to watch it pop, listen to the kernels exploding, smell its unique fragrance, feel its bumpiness in their mouths, and, of course, taste it! Pop up a batch of popcorn for a variety of learning explorations:

✳ Have children scoop some popcorn onto a parachute or a large sheet. Then invite them to grab the edges of the parachute and shake, trying to keep the popcorn from falling off, as they chant *Popcorn, popcorn, pop, pop, pop. Pop like popcorn. Do not stop!*

✳ Let children glue popcorn onto a piece of paper cut into the shape of an ear of corn.

✳ And of course, save some popcorn for eating! Try it with a yummy cheese topping. Simply place popped corn on a microwaveable plate, sprinkle with grated cheddar or mozzarella cheese, and microwave for 15–30 seconds. Cool slightly and enjoy!

Recipe

Corn Chips

These chips are delicious and easy to make!

* 1/2 teaspoon salt
* 1 teaspoon corn oil
* 1/2 cup yellow cornmeal
* 1 3/4 cups boiling water

1. Mix salt, oil, cornmeal, and one cup of the water together in a bowl.

1. Add remaining water and stir. Drop by tablespoons onto a greased cookie sheet.

3. Bake at 425°F for 12-15 minutes until light brown. Cool. Makes two dozen chips.

Be sure to supervise closely for safety—boiling water, of course, must be added by an adult. Let children participate by dividing up the cornmeal and having each child add a spoonful. Children can also take turns mixing the batter and spooning it onto the cookie sheet.

Pop Goes the Kernel!

Give children plastic magnifying glasses and unpopped kernels. Ask, *What do the corn kernels look like?* Try placing a few kernels in a self-sealing bag with some moist soil and leaving it in the sun. When the kernels begin to sprout, plant the seedlings in a pot and measure their growth often.

Many large supermarkets sell popping corn on the cob at this time of year. Put some in the microwave and watch the kernels pop, pop, pop!

Count the Kernels

Shake up some kernels—while building fine-motor skills and math concepts!

Each child (or pair) will need an egg carton with a solid top (no holes), 12 unpopped kernels of corn, and 12 colored sticker dots (four red, four blue, and four yellow).

Place sticker dots randomly on the bottom of each of the 12 egg cups. Have children drop all the kernels into one of the egg cups and close the top. Then invite children to shake the carton! Next, ask children to open their egg cartons and see where the kernels have landed. Ask questions such as:

* *How many kernels are on red?*
* *How many on blue?*
* *How many on yellow?*
* *Does anyone have two kernels in one cup?*
* *How about three or more kernels in one cup?*

After counting, have children place all their kernels back into one cup and repeat. Older children can record the results of each shake by placing a red, blue, and yellow sticker on a piece of paper and making tally marks next to the appropriate color dot.

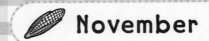

Recipe

Apple Cornbread

Make your own sweet cornbread studded with apples and raisins.

- ✳ 2 tablespoons melted butter
- ✳ 1 egg, beaten
- ✳ 1 cup milk
- ✳ 1/4 cup sugar
- ✳ 1/4 teaspoon ginger
- ✳ 1/4 teaspoon allspice
- ✳ 1/2 teaspoon salt
- ✳ 1 1/2 teaspoons cinnamon
- ✳ 3 1/2 teaspoons baking powder
- ✳ 3/4 cup cornmeal
- ✳ 1 1/4 cups flour
- ✳ 1/2 cup raisins
- ✳ 1 cup apples (a sweet variety), peeled, cored, and chopped

Topping:

- ✳ 1 teaspoon vanilla
- ✳ 1 teaspoon cinnamon
- ✳ 1 tablespoon butter, softened
- ✳ 1/2 cup sugar

1. Beat together butter, egg, milk, and sugar.

2. Mix spices, baking powder, salt, cornmeal, and flour together. Add to the first mixture. Do not overmix.

3. Fold in apples and raisins. Pour into a nine-inch square greased pan.

4. Mix the topping ingredients together until crumbly. Sprinkle on top of batter.

5. Bake at 400°F for 25 minutes.

Cornhusk Wreaths

To make a cornhusk wreath, each child will need:

- ✳ 12-inch cardboard wreath, two to three inches wide
- ✳ thick glue
- ✳ two or three dried ears of miniature corn
- ✳ dried cornhusks (can be purchased at craft stores, or saved from corn on the cob)

1. Have children spread the glue on the cardboard wreaths and press on the husks in any pattern they choose. Children can do this over several days, adding more layers of husks after the ones beneath have dried.

2. Then attach yarn to the mini-corn and tie them onto to the wreaths. Hang the finished wreaths on doors, windows, and walls!

Pop open a good book!

Corn Is Maize by Aliki (HarperCollins, 1996)

Popcorn by Frank Asch (Parent's Press, 1979)

The Popcorn Book by Tomie dePaola (Holiday House, 1978)

Popcorn Dragon by Jane Thayer (William Morrow, 1990)

The Popcorn Shop by Alice Low (Cartwheel, 1993)

Tractor by Craig Brown (Greenwillow, 1995)

Baking Bread

Bread baking is a wonderful tactile process that helps children develop their fine and gross motor skills while engaging all five senses. It allows them the freedom to poke, pinch, and pound—and they can eat their creations! They love the silky feel of the flour, the magic of the bubbly yeast, the warmth of the dough, and the physical process of kneading. They also enjoy giving their finished edible creation to a friend or relative! When you bake bread with children, you'll help them develop awareness of different cultures, safety skills, cooperation, and clean-up skills. At the same time you'll be teaching nutrition, science, and new vocabulary.

Bread, Bread, Bread

Bread comes in all sizes, shapes, and flavors—and from all corners of the world! Share Ann Morris' wonderful book, *Bread, Bread, Bread* (HarperTrophy, 1993), then take a field trip to a grocery store or bakery. How many different types of bread can children find? Let them choose several that are new to them to bring back.

Baking 101

Some tips as you embark on your kitchen adventures:

✳ Establish a regular day for baking, whether it's once a week or once a month.

✳ Start with simple yeast and quick breads.

✳ Add to your repertoire by asking children's families—and your friends and relatives—for favorite bread recipes. Start your own bread cookbook!

✳ Be flexible. Loaves can be long and lean, short and fat, freeform or neat rounds and rectangles. Some children will be happy to plop dough into a pan, others may want to roll it into a baguette shape.

✳ Be creative. Try baking bread on a pizza stone or a cookie sheet, or in a flower pot or coffee can!

✳ Allow for individual creativity. Have children paint their creations with milk or egg glaze, and sprinkle with poppy seeds, sesame seeds, parmesan cheese, sugar or sprinkles, or salt.

✳ Experiment. Try substituting a small amount of wheat germ for some of the flour, or add nonfat dry milk to fortify your loaf.

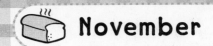

Recipe

Golden Harvest Bread

Bake a double batch of this delicious, not-too-sweet quick bread for your harvest baskets (page 52)! Seal in plastic wrap, let children wrap in colored tissue paper, and tie with a ribbon.

(yield: six or seven three-by six-inch loaves.)

* 2/3 cup corn oil
* 1/3 cup maple syrup
* 2 eggs
* 2 cups cooked butternut squash (you can substitute sweet potato, pumpkin, or carrot)
* 1/2 teaspoon cloves
* 1 teaspoon cinnamon
* 1 teaspoon nutmeg
* 1 teaspoon salt
* 1 tablespoon baking soda
* 1 1/3 cup whole wheat flour
* 2 cups white flour
* 2 cups chopped walnuts
* 2 cups chopped cranberries

1. Mix oil, syrup, eggs, and squash well.

2. Mix together remaining ingredients and add to first mixture.

3. Bake at 350°F for 40 minutes in greased mini-loaf pans. Cool 10 minutes, then remove from pan.

Recipe

Bread Sculpture

This bread is just for play! Children enjoy pinching, poking, and rolling free-form sculptures or creating a handprint that will serve as a keepsake for many years to come.

* 1/2 cup salt
* 3/4 cup hot water
* 1 tablespoon oil
* 2 cups whole wheat flour

1. Mix salt and water together to dissolve salt. Add oil and flour and mix thoroughly.

2. Children can make free-form sculptures, or roll dough out into circles 1/3 inch thick, and press in their hand prints!

3. Dry in 150°F oven for one to two hours, turning once. These can be left natural or painted. Makes two cups or two hand plaques.

Knead It!

Kneading helps develop the gluten in your bread. It's also an easy-to-teach technique! Have children fold the dough in front of them, push it down with the heel of their hand, and then turn the dough clockwise. Continue to fold, push and turn for five minutes until the dough becomes springy, elastic and smooth. Very young children can simply pound and turn the dough over occasionally.

Recipe

Bread in a Bag

Kids love this unique, fun, and fast recipe. They can even personalize their loaves by adding one special ingredient to their bags.

 ❈ 1 packet yeast

 ❈ 1 teaspoon salt

 ❈ 3 tablespoons sugar

 ❈ 3 tablespoons nonfat dry milk

 ❈ 4 tablespoons wheat germ

 ❈ 1 1/2 cups white flour

 ❈ 3 tablespoons olive oil

 ❈ 1 cup hot water

 ❈ 1 1/4 cups whole wheat flour

"Children's choice" ingredients: walnuts, sunflower seeds, pumpkin seeds, raisins, dried cranberries, dried cherries, cinnamon, chocolate chips, shredded coconut

1. Give each child his or her own resealable bag (the ingredients list above is for each bag). Place the specified amounts of yeast, salt, sugar, dry milk, wheat germ, and flour in each bag and have children shake, shake, shake!

2. Add oil and water to bags, and mix by squishing. Add flour and knead bags well. Invite children to choose a handful of one or two ingredients to knead in.

3. Place dough onto greased pans (you can also divide each bag into thirds for miniature loaves). Let rise for thirty minutes in a warm place.

4. Bake at 375°F for 25 minutes. (Each bag makes one large loaf or three miniature loaves.)

Recipe

Pueblo Sunflower Seed Bread

Kids love patting out these easy flat breads! Eat them warm and soft from the oven, or enjoy them crisp the next day, like a cracker. The aromatic rounds are great with peanut butter or sliced cheese!

 ❈ 1/2 cup unsalted raw sunflower seeds

 ❈ 1/2 teaspoon salt

 ❈ 2 teaspoons baking powder

 ❈ 1 tablespoon brown sugar

 ❈ 1 tablespoon butter

 ❈ 1 1/2 cup whole wheat flour

 ❈ 1/2 cup water

1. Grind sunflower seeds in food processor until fine. Add salt, baking power, brown sugar, butter, and flour and pulse several times, adding the water as you go.

2. Continue until dough forms into ball (add one or two more tablespoons of water if necessary). Divide dough into eight pieces and pat or roll each into a five-inch circle.

3. Bake eight minutes at 400°F on ungreased cookie sheet or pizza stone. Store in resealable bag. Makes eight five-inch flatbreads.

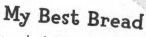
Recipe

Bread Stick Twists

Bake up a batch of these Italian bread sticks (or *grissini*) for a yummy snack! For very young children who can't yet do the twisting, simple shapes, letters or cookie-cutter shapes work just as well.

* 1 packet yeast
* 1 cup warm water
* 2 tablespoons salt
* 2 tablespoons sugar
* 2 tablespoons butter
* 1 cup warm milk
* 2 cups whole wheat flour
* 4 1/2 cups white flour

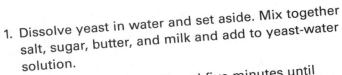

1. Dissolve yeast in water and set aside. Mix together salt, sugar, butter, and milk and add to yeast-water solution.

2. Add flour and mix in. Knead five minutes until smooth and elastic. Place in oiled bowl, cover, and let rise in warm place for one hour.

3. Punch down and roll into a 10- by 24-inch rectangle. Cut into 1/2-inch strips.

4. Show children how to pick up ends of strips in one hand, grab the middle with the other hand, stretch, twist and pinch ends together.

5. Lay on greased baking sheet and let sit 15 minutes. Brush with beaten egg white and sprinkle with salt or sesame seeds.

6. Bake at 425°F for 15 minutes or until golden. Makes 3 1/2 dozen 10-inch sticks.

My Best Bread

Let each child bring his or her favorite bread to share one day. Talk about the basic ingredients that most breads have in common. You might set out some white flour, whole wheat flour, cornmeal, yeast, baking soda, and salt on small paper plates and pass each around. Invite children to explore the different textures!

Book Nook

Open a book and watch children's interest level rise!

Seven Loaves of Bread by Ferida Wolff (Tambourine Books, 1993)

The Sleeping Bread by Stefan Czernecki (Hyperion, 1992)

This Is The Bread I Baked For Ned by Crescent Dragonwagon (Macmillan, 1989)

The Little Red Hen by Paul Galdone (Clarion, 1985)

Turkey Time

The turkey's a funny-looking bird! If possible, take children to a nearby farm or zoo to see a real turkey. Ask questions such as: *How many toes does a turkey have? What do turkeys eat? Can turkeys fly?* If you are lucky, you might even hear the turkey make its gobble-gobble call or see it spread its tail feathers in a proud display. Don't forget to bring a camera!

Fun Turkey Facts

✳ Most domestic turkeys are so heavy they are unable to fly!

✳ Wild turkeys (*Meleagris gallopavo*) live in woods in parts of North America and are the largest game birds found in this part of the world. They eat acorns, seeds, small insects, and wild berries.

✳ Peacocks aren't the only ones who show off! Male turkeys puff up their bodies and spread their tail feathers (just like a peacock).

✳ Female turkeys lay tan and speckled brown eggs—as many as 18 at a time! It takes about a month for them to hatch.

✳ When the babies (known as poults) hatch, they stay with their mother all year.

✳ Wild turkeys have dark feathers for camouflage. The bare skin on their throats and head changes color from gray to bright red or blue when they are upset or excited!

✳ A female turkey is called a hen. A male turkey is a tom or a gobbler.

Turkey Tag

This game will keep children warm as they play in the brisk November air.

Make a turkey tail by cutting feather shapes from colored construction paper. Laminate the feathers, fan them out, and staple together at the base to make a tail. Then choose a child to be the first turkey and attach the tail feathers to the child's back pocket, pants waistband, or belt with heavy duty tape. The first person to tag the tail feathers gets to be the next turkey. Continue until each child has had a chance to wear the turkey's tail.

Six Big Turkeys

Here is a lively, rhyming Thanksgiving chant to recite with children. Children can also act out the chant!

Six big turkeys, "gobble, gobble," they cry,
One waddles off, now there are five.
Five big turkeys by the barn door,
One waddles off, now there are four.
Four big turkeys under a tree,
One waddles off, now there are three.
Three big turkeys, nothing to do,
One waddles off, now there are two.
Two big turkeys in the noonday sun,
One waddles off, now there is one.
One big turkey, better run away,
Find other turkeys to play with all day!

Turkey Talk

Many people eat turkey at Thanksgiving, but some people do not eat meat. Explain what *vegetarian* means and talk about other types of protein-rich foods that might substitute for turkey at the Thanksgiving table. More than 200 years ago, when our country was new, the eagle was chosen to be a symbol of the United States, but Ben Franklin thought the turkey would be a better choice. Invite children to take a look at the eagle on a dollar bill. Which bird would they have chosen?

Pin the Feathers

Try this twist on *Pin the Tail on the Donkey* for a game that children will gobble right up!

Cut a turkey shape from felt and cut a felt feather for each child. Write children's names on the feathers using fabric paint. Then let children decorate their feathers by gluing on glitter and small colorful feathers (available at craft stores).

When children's feathers are dry, place the turkey on a feltboard and play *Pin the Feather on the Turkey*. Cover children's eyes and let them take turns trying to attach their feathers to the turkey's body. You can keep the feltboard, turkey and feathers out all week for an ongoing game. At the end of the week, let children take their feathers home.

Book Nook

Gobble up a good turkey tale!

All About Turkeys by Jim Arnosky (Scholastic, 1998)

Gracias, the Thanksgiving Turkey by Joy Cowley (Scholastic, 1996)

Sometimes It's Turkey, Sometimes It's Feathers by Lorna Balian (Abingdon, 1973)

Turk and Runt by Lisa Wheeler (Atheneum, 2002)

A Turkey for Thanksgiving by Eve Bunting (Clarion, 1991)

Turkey on the Loose by Sylvie Wickstrom (Dial, 1990)

One Potato, Two Potato...

Have a potato-tasting. Pass around several types of potatoes (sweet, Idaho, red, and so on) and have children examine them. How are they the same? How are they different? Chop (leave skins on for identification), boil, and let cool. Have children choose their favorite, graph the results, then use that type to make mashed potatoes!

Mashed Potatoes

* 8 large potatoes (any variety)
* 1 stick butter
* 1/2 cup milk
* 2 teaspoons salt
* 1/2 teaspoon pepper

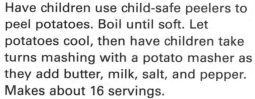

Have children use child-safe peelers to peel potatoes. Boil until soft. Let potatoes cool, then have children take turns mashing with a potato masher as they add butter, milk, salt, and pepper. Makes about 16 servings.

Wobble Wobble Gobble

Try this movement poem.

The turkey is a funny bird,
(tuck hands in armpits, strut, flap "wings")

His head goes wobble, wobble.
(wobble head forward and back)

But all he says is just one word:
Gobble, gobble, gobble!
(strut, flap, wobble, and gobble)

—Annie Stiefel

Thanksgiving Fun

Thanksgiving is a special time. Together we feast, give thanks, and carry on family and cultural traditions. Children will feel the holiday spirit by as they prepare traditional foods and make decorations. Take the time with children to pause, appreciate, and give thanks.

Set the Thanksgiving Table

Children can make beautiful decorations to bring home to their own tables.

✳ For napkin holders, cut paper towel rolls into one-inch pieces. Have children glue on lace, fabric scraps, colored tissue paper bits, glitter, or stickers.

✳ Make tie-dyed napkins by boiling cranberries in water (supervise children closely for safety). Fasten rubber bands in several areas on squares of cotton (handkerchiefs work well), soak for several hours, and dry!

✳ Have children cut pictures from old magazines that show things they are thankful for, then glue them onto construction paper. Help children label the items, then laminate to create placemats.

Apple Pomanders

Children enjoy the scent of apples, cloves, cinnamon, and allspice as they make this old-fashioned holiday gift. If you start them during Thanksgiving week, they will be dry and ready to bring home in time for the December holidays!

1. Each child needs a small apple, a handful of whole cloves, a large button, and a piece of colored ribbon. For every 8 to 10 pomanders, you will also need two ounces each of ground cinnamon, ground cloves, and allspice (available in bulk at health food stores).

2. Let each child choose a button and an apple. Thread a large doll needle (available at fabric stores) and use it to loop the ribbon through the button. Then push the needle through the bottom of the apple. Next, have children press the cloves into the apple until it is well covered. Use permanent marker to write children's initials on the buttons.

3. Place the apples in a shoe box, let children sprinkle with six ounces of ground spices, and cover. Turn the apples over once a week until dry and light in weight (about three to six weeks). Remove from box, brush off excess spice, and wrap in tissue paper. These are great to hang in a closet, kitchen, or car!

Giving Thanks Around the World

Almost every culture around the world has a harvest festival to give thanks for the year's bounty. Many also have a ritual to ensure a good growing season for the coming year. How do children of other countries celebrate the harvest? Take a trip to the library to find out.

Harvest Baskets

Children enjoy presenting this at their own harvest feast!

Each child needs a 42-ounce oatmeal container (with paper peeled off). Cut as shown above to create the basket shape, and staple the handle together. Let children paint the basket with Mod Podge (found at craft supply stores) and add colorful leaves, tissue paper, or fabric scraps for decoration.

Next, help children line their baskets with paper leaves. They can fill their finished baskets with nuts, small fruits, and other offerings, and share with family and friends. Or, donate a gift basket to a local shelter, soup kitchen, or senior citizen home.

Recipe

Cranberry Nut Bread

These mini-loaves are the perfect child-size contribution to the Thanksgiving table!

* ❊ 1/2 cup very soft butter
* ❊ 1 3/4 cups white or brown sugar
* ❊ 1 3/4 cups orange juice
* ❊ 2 eggs, beaten
* ❊ 1/4 teaspoon nutmeg
* ❊ 1 teaspoon salt
* ❊ 1 teaspoon baking soda
* ❊ 1 tablespoon baking powder
* ❊ 5 cups flour
* ❊ 2 tablespoons grated orange rind
* ❊ 2 cups chopped walnuts
* ❊ 3 1/2 cups chopped fresh cranberries

1. Mix butter, sugar, juice, and eggs.

2. Mix together nutmeg, salt, baking soda, baking powder, and flour, and add to first mixture.

3. Fold in the orange rind, walnuts, and cranberries.

4. Pour into two large greased loaf pans (or muffin tins) and let stand for 20 minutes.

5. Bake at 350°F for one hour. Makes six mini-loaves or two dozen muffins.

Book Nook

Give thanks for books with these holiday titles.

Hardscrabble Harvest by Dahlov Ipcar (Doubleday, 1976)

It's Thanksgiving! by Jack Prelutsky (William Morrow, 1982)

Mousekin's Thanksgiving by Edna Miller (Prentice Hall, 1985)

One Little, Two Little, Three Little Pilgrims by Barbara Hennessy (Viking, 1999)

Over the River and Through the Woods by Lydia Marie Child (Scholastic, 1996)

Thanksgiving Memories

Holidays can come and go all too quickly. If your program is in session the day after Thanksgiving, invite children to bring in one of their favorite foods left over from their Thanksgiving meal for snack. Ask: *Did everyone bring the same food?* Talk about ways in which people and families can be the same and different. Invite children to share Thanksgiving memories by asking:

* ❊ Where did you celebrate Thanksgiving this year?

* ❊ With whom did you celebrate Thanksgiving?

* ❊ Do you celebrate Thanksgiving in the same place each year?

* ❊ What is your favorite Thanksgiving food?

Happy Holidays

The winter holidays are magical, exciting times for children. They see their home and community decorated with twinkling lights, stars, bows, and colorful candy. They hear holiday music and stories. They taste and smell traditional dishes and treats.

Cultural Celebrations

The holidays present a wealth of opportunities for expanding children's knowledge of people and places around the world. Children can learn about and enjoy their own customs and traditions, as well as some that are not so familiar. As young children are exposed to cultural diversity, they develop awareness and respect for our differences.

There are plenty of fascinating customs and celebrations to choose from this season: Hanukkah (the Jewish Festival of Lights); the Feast of St. Nicholas (celebrated in Europe); the Mexican tradition of Las Posadas; the African-American celebration of Kwanzaa; plus a variety of New Year's customs from around the world. You can bring different cultures into your classroom all season long. Add a Mexican piñata to your holiday party. Make tree ornaments. Serve Hanukkah latkes (potato pancakes) and spin a dreidel. Make a felt board kinara (candle holder) to celebrate Kwanzaa. Then, as the new year approaches, help children learn how different cultures celebrate! For instance, in Hungary it's good luck to touch a pig on New Year's Day, in Puerto Rico it's customary to throw water out of windows, in Spain, people eat a grape each time the clock chimes at midnight. Try to incorporate one or two new customs or foods into your program at this special time of year!

The Tradition of Giving

The holiday time is also a perfect opportunity to help children learn about the importance of giving and sharing. Invite them to experience the excitement and pride of giving a handmade gift to a loved one. You can also encourage children to share the holiday spirit with people in your community. Take some of your baked goodies to a senior citizens' home, ask each child to bring a can of food or a new toy from home to donate to a shelter, or send homemade cards to a hospital.

R & R

In the midst of the holiday bustle, it's important to leave enough time for some rest and relaxation. With community functions, holiday parties, shopping for gifts, and family gatherings, the calendar can begin to look like an overworked crossword puzzle! Slow the holiday season down by penciling in at least one morning or afternoon a week for some much-needed rest and relaxation, such as a laid-back morning spent sipping cocoa or an afternoon spent reading favorite books.

Let children burn off some of their pre-holiday excitement by making an obstacle course in your playroom, using whatever equipment you have on hand. Put some masking tape strips on the floor for jumping across. Hang hula-hoops for a balloon toss.

However you celebrate, the holiday season brings special opportunities for giving, sharing, and learning to your classroom!

The Joy of Giving

Part of the excitement of the holiday season is the fun of giving and receiving presents. Take time to help children create gifts to give to the special people in their lives. Give them the opportunity to make and wrap presents, surprise their loved ones, and feel the pleasure of giving.

Recipe

Cinnamon Ornaments

This is a lovely gift for a parent or grandparent.

* ❋ 1 tablespoon ground cloves
* ❋ 2 tablespoons water
* ❋ 3 tablespoons white glue
* ❋ 3/4 cup applesauce
* ❋ 1 cup cinnamon (buy in bulk at a spice or health food store)

Mix all ingredients together until dough has a clay-like consistency (add one or two more tablespoons of water if it's too dry). Next, dust a work surface with cinnamon and roll out the dough to 1/4-inch thick. Have children cut out ornaments using holiday cookie cutters. Help children poke a hole in each ornament with a straw, then let ornaments dry on baking racks. String with ribbon. Makes approximately four dozen two-inch ornaments.

It's Snowing!

No matter what climate you live in, children will enjoy creating (and giving) this beautiful snow globe.

For each child, you will need a clean, empty baby food jar and lid, a two-inch evergreen sprig, and a teaspoon-sized ball of oil-based clay. Have children stick the clay to the inside of the jar lid, then stick the evergreen sprig upright in the clay. Next, help them place a tablespoon of glitter in the bottom of the jar and fill the jar with water.

Run a bead of hot glue around the rim of the jar, then screw on the lid (of course, only an adult should do this step). When the glue has set, shake it up and let it snow!

Recipe

3-D Paint

This homemade puffy paint is perfect for decorating holiday greeting cards and crafts. For one cup of paint, you'll need:

* ✳ 1/3 cup kosher salt
* ✳ 1/3 cup flour
* ✳ 4 1/2 tablespoons water
* ✳ 2 tablespoons liquid tempera paint (any color)

Mix ingredients together well, and place the mixture in small squeeze bottles (use the empty travel-size containers available in drugstores). Let children create three-dimensional paintings by squeezing the paint onto lightweight cardboard or posterboard. They can also sprinkle their paintings with glitter before they dry. The paint will puff up, then harden!

Wrap It Up!

Help children label and wrap their gifts. For simple, inexpensive gift wrap, supply children with holiday-theme cookie cutters and sponges. Have them dip the cutters and sponges into paint, and press onto newsprint.

If you made apple pomanders in November (see page 52), wrap them as holiday gifts. Let the ribbon dangle outside the wrapping so that it can be hung on a holiday tree.

Gingerbread Memo Pads

1. Give each child a 10- to 12-inch gingerbread boy or girl cut from lightweight cardboard, a self-stick magnet, and a three-inch square pad of sticky notes. Set out brown tempera paint, wallpaper or gift wrap scraps, glue, scissors and yarn.

2. Have children paint the gingerbread cutouts and let dry. Then punch holes around the edges of the gingerbread figures and have children lace the holes with yarn.

3. Next, let each child choose a piece of wallpaper or gift wrap. Use it to cut a simple dress or overalls for each gingerbread boy or girl. Then have children glue on the clothing and glue the notepad in the center. Attach a self-stick magnet to the back of each to brighten any refrigerator!

Recipe

Yummy Fruitcake

Zucchini provides an updated twist on traditional fruitcake. This moist, colorful treat gets better with time!

- ❉ 1 tablespoon vanilla
- ❉ 1 cup corn oil
- ❉ 2 cups packed brown sugar
- ❉ 3 eggs
- ❉ 1/2 teaspoon baking powder
- ❉ 2 teaspoons baking soda
- ❉ 3 cups flour
- ❉ 1 teaspoon salt
- ❉ 1 teaspoon cloves
- ❉ 1 teaspoon nutmeg
- ❉ 2 teaspoons allspice
- ❉ 1 tablespoon cinnamon
- ❉ 1 cup currants
- ❉ 1 cup chopped walnuts
- ❉ 1 cup dried cranberries
- ❉ 1 cup dried apricots, chopped
- ❉ 2 cups shredded zucchini

1. Mix together vanilla, oil, brown sugar, and eggs.

2. Mix together baking powder, baking soda, flour, salt, and spices well and stir into the first mixture.

3. Stir in the currants, walnuts, cranberries, apricots, and zucchini. Pour mixture into six small greased loaf pans or two large loaf pans. Bake at 325°F for 65 minutes.

4. Cool in pans. Remove and wrap well in plastic wrap. Store in refrigerator or freezer at least two weeks before serving.

Talk About Giving

As children create their gifts, ask questions such as:

Do you like surprises? Why or why not?

Why do people give presents?

Why do you think we wrap presents?

Have you ever given a gift before? How did it make you feel?

What is the best gift you ever received?

What is the best gift you have ever given?

Book Nook

A book is a gift you can open again and again! Here are some to enjoy:

Giving by Shirley Hughes (Candlewick, 1993)

Happy Birthday, Moon by Frank Asch (Prentice Hall, 1982)

Mr. Rabbit and the Lovely Present by Charlotte Zolotow (Harper & Row, 1962)

No Roses for Harry by Gene Zion (HarperCollins, 1958)

The Present by Ed Emberley (Little Brown, 1991)

Something from Nothing by Phoebe Gilman (Scholastic, 1992)

Hats Off!

As colder weather settles in, it's time for the hats to come out! Talk about the hats that people in your community, such as police officers, fire fighters, chefs, and construction workers, wear. Discuss the types of hats that kings and queens, clowns, magicians, and baseball players wear. Compare the hats and talk about how they are the same and different. Try wearing a different hat as you greet children each day!

Newspaper Hats

Make your own folded newspaper hats (see diagrams below). Let children help fold the newspaper and hold it steady while you secure it with tape or staples. Then have them paint their hats with tempera paints. When dry, print children's names on the hats. You might later share *Martin's Hats* by Joan Blos (William Morrow, 1984) as children wear their hats.

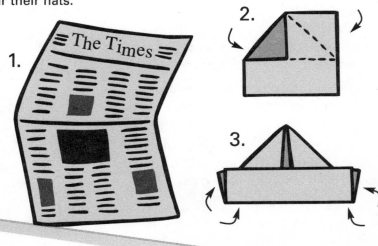

Show & Share

Ask each child to wear a hat—any type of hat—to school. At circle time, read *Whose Hat?* by Margaret Miller (Greenwillow, 1988). Afterward, give each child a chance to talk about the hat he or she is wearing. Get them started with questions such as *What might you build wearing your hard hat?* or *What would be a perfect place to wear your hat?*

Musical Hats

Invite children to sing this song (to the tune of Yankee Doodle) several times into a tape recorder:

When the wind blows round and round,
up and down and all around,
When the wind blows round and round,
you know it is hat weather!

Then play a game of musical hats! Place one hat per child in a large circle on the floor and play the recording as children march around the outside of the circle. When you stop the music, each child sits down next to the nearest hat and put it on his or her head. (There's no need to remove a hat after each round— children will enjoy simply trying on a different hat each time!)

Hats, Hats, Hats

Ask family members, community workers, and organizations for hat donations. You can also check yard sales, used clothing stores, and uniform supply stores. Child-size versions of community worker hats are available in school supply and toy catalogs. To make adult-size hats fit children's heads, simply stuff the insides with soft crumpled paper! Make your hat collection readily available so that children can easily incorporate them into their dramatic play. A shelf, tabletop, or box will work well, but a short hat rack is even more inviting!

59

Hat Parade

Provide children with dress-up clothes, let each child choose an outfit, then invite them to choose a hat from your collection. Then parade around the room (or outdoors if weather permits)! Choose a child to be the parade leader and give him or her a instrument to beat out a marching rhythm. You can play recorded marching music, too. Let each child have a turn being the leader. This is a great opportunity to take photos!

Caps for Sale

Share the beloved classic *Caps for Sale* by Esphyr Slobodkina (HarperCollins, 1947), then make some caps of your own.

Cut out the center of an eight-inch paper plate for each child and place the plate rim over a five-inch paper bowl. Then tape or staple the plate and bowl together to make a cap. To match the colors of caps in the story, set out brown, gray, blue, and red paint and let each child choose one color to paint his or her hat. When hats are dry, read *Caps for Sale* again, this time letting one child play the peddler as the rest of the group plays the monkeys! (A wonderful video version of *Caps for Sale* is available through Weston Woods, 800-243-5020.)

Hat Talk

As you explore hats with children, ask questions such as:

* *Why do we wear hats?*
* *How many different kinds of hats can you think of?*
* *What kinds of hats protect us from the weather?*
* *What kinds of hats keep people safe at work or play?*
* *How are a hat and a hood the same? How are they different?*
* *Do you have a favorite hat? Tell us about it.*

Book Nook

Put on your storytelling hat and open one of these books.

Hats, Hats, Hats by Ann Morris (Lothrop, 1989)

Ho for a Hat by William Jay Smith (Little Brown, 1989)

Which Hat Is That? by Anna Grossnickle Hines (Harcourt, 2002)

Who Took the Farmer's Hat? by Joan Nodset (HarperCollins, 1988)

Zoe's Hats by Sharon Lane Holm (Boyds Mills, 2003)

Winter Is Coming

Children associate the changing of the seasons not only with the weather, but also with the events, holidays, and traditions that take place. Depending on where you live, children may have already rolled their first snowballs, but winter officially begins on or around the 21st of December, the shortest day of the year.

Light the Menorah & Kinara

The menorah is the traditional candelabrum that Jews light on Hanukkah. One candle is lit on the first night, two on the second night, and so on, until the eighth night. The middle candle is lit each night and is used to light the others.

Menorah

Many African Americans light the candles of the kinara each night of Kwanzaa, which starts on December 26th and ends on January 1st. The black candle in the center represents the African-American people. The three red candles on the right symbolize struggle, and the three green candles on the left signify hope for the future.

Kinara

You can make a flannel board kinara and menorah and "light" the candles in your classroom. Cut a kinara and a menorah shape from felt. Then cut flames out of yellow or orange felt, and candles in the appropriate colors (Hanukkah candles can be any color). Glue a strip of sandpaper to the back of the candles for durability. Place the menorah and kinara on a flannel board and let children take turns "lighting" the candles each day during the seven days of Kwanzaa and the eight days of Hanukkah.

The Snowman

Teach children the following fingerplay:

I made a great big snowman,
(raise hands to the ceiling)

He was very round and fat,
(hold arms in a circle in front of tummy)

He had a carrot for a nose,
(put finger on nose)

And a big [any color] hat!
(form triangle with arms above head)

Along came a bunny,
(hold two fingers in a V shape)

A very hungry bunny,
Who was looking for some lunch.
(rub tummy)

He ate my snowman's nose off,
(open and close fingers)

Nibble, nibble, CRUNCH!
(pantomime biting with teeth)

—Annie Stiefel

1. After reciting the fingerplay, invite children to make their own paper snow people. Provide each child with two-inch, four-inch, and five-inch white paper circles, cut-outs of hats and carrots, wiggle eyes, assorted buttons, and glue sticks. Children can glue their snowpeople onto dark construction paper.

2. Next, depending on where you live, you might also make a real snowman outside. Create a multicolored snowman with spray bottles filled with colored water!

Hands & Feet Reindeer

Help pairs of children trace each other's hands, forearms, and feet onto brown construction paper, then cut out the shapes and glue together as shown. You might point out to children that each reindeer resembles the letter Y. Invite children to give wiggle eyes and a red pompom nose to their reindeer.

Snip a Snowflake

Celebrate winter's arrival by making some snowflakes.

For each child, fold a basket-style paper coffee filter in half, and then fold the resulting semicircle in thirds so that they end up with a shape like a pizza slice. Have children snip small V shapes from all the edges, and then unfold their snowflakes. Have children brush their completed snowflakes with sparkle paint (see 63). Let the snowflakes dry and hang them in windows, from ceilings, or on a tree.

Match & Snack Mittens

1. Have children toss all their mittens into a basket (if you live in a region where children don't wear mittens, play this game with socks). Then have one or two children match all the mittens. Point out that when two children work together, the job is easier!

2. After sorting and matching, create some edible mittens! Using a batch of your favorite sugar cookie dough, let each child cut out four or six mittens with a mitten-shaped cookie cutter. If you don't have a mitten cookie cutter, create a few templates out of cardboard. Children can trace around the templates with plastic knives.

3. While cookies are baking, make milk icing (two tablespoons sweetened condensed milk, colored with several drops of food coloring). Use an empty egg carton for a paint palette, placing a different color icing in each cup. Have children paint two cookies each (with clean brushes) to match their mittens or a friend's mittens. Children can use candy-covered chocolates for dots.

4. Display all the cookies and invite children to find their matching pair and show it to the group before eating!

Sparkle Paint

This paint is easy to make, and creates a magical effect: it makes anything sparkle in the light.

Bring one cup of water to a boil and stir in one cup of Epsom salt (supervise children closely). Continue stirring until salt is dissolved, and let cool.

Then paint! Remember that sparkle paint works its magic when dry, so allow a few moments after painting for the sparkle effect to appear. It shows up best on colored paper (if using white paper, add a drop or two of food coloring to the mixture). As children paint, use new words such as *sparkle*, *glisten*, *twinkle*, *crystals*, and *glint* in conversation.

Santa Pops!

Teach children the following fingerplay (first, draw a little three-dot Santa face on your thumb).

Here is the chimney,
(make a fist with thumb tucked in)

Here is the top.
(place other hand, flat, palm down, on top of fist)

Open it up,
(remove hand on top)

And out Santa pops!
(pop thumb up)

—Annie Stiefel

Draw a Santa face on children's thumbs with non-toxic marker, and have them do the motions themselves as you recite the words together.

Six Little Mittens

At circle time, recite and act out the following poem, inserting a different name for each verse.

Six little mittens hanging to dry,

[Child's name] came and took one, now there are five.

Five little mittens frozen to the core,

[Child's name] came and took one, now there are four.

Four little mittens as clean as could be,

[Child's name] came and took one, now there are three.

Three little mittens waiting for WHO?

[Child's name] came and took one, now there are two.

Two little mittens warmed by the sun,

[Child's name] came and took one, now there is one.

One little mitten, looking for its match,

[Child's name] came and took one, and that is THAT!

Book Nook

Cozy up with a good book!

Beni's First Chanukah by Jane Breskin Zalben (Holt, 1988)

Celebrating Kwanzaa by Diane Hoyt-Goldsmith (Holiday House, 1993)

Just in Time for Christmas by Louise Borden (Scholastic, 1994)

Las Posadas: An Hispanic Christmas Celebration by Diane Hoyt-Goldsmith (Holiday House, 1999)

The Mitten by Jan Brett (Putnam, 1989)

The Night Before Christmas by Clement C. Moore (Knopf, 1984)

Owl Moon by Jane Yolen (Philomel, 1987)

The Polar Express by Chris Van Allsburg (Houghton Mifflin, 1985)

Winter Across America by Seymour Simon (Hyperion, 1994)

Winter Poems by Barbara Rogasky (Scholastic, 1994)

Get Out There!

Many animals hibernate during the winter, but people don't! Talk to children about the importance of getting fresh air, exercise, and sunshine in the winter months. You might have children put a sticker on the calendar for each day the group is able to play outside—even if it's just for a few minutes. On days you're stuck indoors, discuss hibernation. Add blankets and pillows to the dramatic play center so children can pretend to hibernate!

Gingerbread Extravaganza

Everyone loves a gingerbread house! Mixing, baking, assembling, and decorating a gingerbread house is easier than you might think, especially if you plan it over the course of several days. Children will enjoy seeing their house take shape, and adding their own creative touches. Plus, ginger smells great!

Gingerbread History

People have been making gingerbread in Western Europe in one form or another since the 12th century. Germany is the country with the oldest, strongest gingerbread tradition. In the United States, the making of gingerbread dates back to colonial days.

Spice It Up!

Explore ginger and other spices:

※ Show children crystallized ginger and powdered ginger. How are they the same? How are they different? How do you suppose the powdered ginger is made?

※ Put spices in empty film cylinders (one spice per cylinder): cinnamon, ginger, nutmeg, and cloves. Pass them around one at a time and tell children which spice they are smelling. Then pass one around and have children guess which it is.

※ Ginger has long been a staple of the Asian diet. On a globe, show children the countries in which the most ginger is grown: Jamaica, India, Africa, and China.

Gingerbread House

Recipe

1. Make the Dough

Children can help you measure and mix.

* ❄ 1 cup butter, melted
* ❄ 1 cup sugar
* ❄ 1 1/4 cups molasses
* ❄ 2 eggs
* ❄ 1 teaspoon salt
* ❄ 1 teaspoon baking soda
* ❄ 1 teaspoon cloves
* ❄ 1 teaspoon nutmeg
* ❄ 1 tablespoon ginger
* ❄ 1 tablespoon cinnamon
* ❄ 6 cups flour

1. Mix butter, sugar, molasses, and eggs.

2. Mix together the dry ingredients, add to wet ingredients, and mix again.

3. On a floured surface, roll dough into a 3/4-inch thick rectangle and wrap in plastic wrap. Refrigerate for at least one hour (keep chilled until you are ready to continue).

2. Bake It!

1. Begin by drawing house templates on cardboard, using the diagrams (see below left) as a guide. Have children help you measure out each piece. Cut out and label each template piece (roof, roof, front, back, side, side). Use the cardboard to show children how the house will be constructed.

2. Next, roll out the dough to 1/4-inch thick on a floured surface. Then lay the house templates on the dough and cut around them using a pizza wheel or a plastic knife. Carefully cut out the doorframe and windows, saving the cut-out pieces to make shutters and a door. You should have six pieces of dough, excluding the shutter and door cutouts. Save and refrigerate all the leftover dough for cookies (see page 68).

3. When you have finished cutting, slide a large spatula under the dough. Slide each piece carefully onto a greased cookie sheet and bake at 350°F for eight minutes. While pieces are still warm, place the original cardboard templates on them and trim the edges of the walls and roof so that they are straight. Then return to oven for 4 to 6 more minutes. Cool on a flat surface, then cover.

As the dough bakes, read a book from the Book Nook (page 68) together!

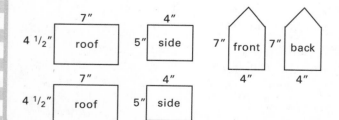

3. Build It!

1. Now assemble your gingerbread house. Cover a board, tray, or piece of heavy-duty corrugated cardboard with foil or holiday wrapping paper to serve as a base.

2. Next, fill a small self-sealing plastic bag with Royal Icing (see recipe below). Snip off at one corner so you can squeeze icing out. Starting with the back wall piece, pipe icing onto the bottom edge and along one side edge, and adhere the wall to the house base. Repeat with each wall, adhering it to the edge of the previous wall with icing. Squeeze each joint snug and square as you go along. When all four walls are in place, let icing harden for 10 minutes.

3. Pipe icing on the peak ends of the house and along the roof line of one roof piece. Then place both roof halves on the house and hold them in place for several minutes to set. Let icing harden for 10 minutes.

4. Pipe icing onto the house for decoration. Let children add shutters, door and candies to decorate the house, using the icing as glue. If making cookies (see below), you might stand some of the gingerbread boys, girls, Santas, reindeer, and trees around the house, gluing them in place with icing. Sift a fresh snowfall of confectioner's sugar over the scene to complete the display. Admire for up to a week, then eat!

Royal Icing

Use this icing to assemble and decorate your gingerbread house.

- ❋ 2 tablespoons meringue powder (sold with baking supplies)
- ❋ 1 pound confectioner's sugar
- ❋ 1 teaspoon vanilla or lemon extract
- ❋ 6 tablespoons warm water

Beat all ingredients together for 10 minutes until stiff peaks form.

Gingerbread Biscuits

If you don't have time to make a gingerbread house, here are some quick and easy biscuits. They're great warm, with butter or cream cheese!

* 1/2 teaspoon cinnamon
* 1/2 teaspoon cloves
* 1/2 teaspoon salt
* 1 teaspoon ginger
* 1 teaspoon baking soda
* 1/4 cup sugar
* 2 cups flour
* 1/4 cup molasses
* 1/2 cup milk

1. Mix dry ingredients together.

2. Mix molasses and milk together and add to dry ingredients, mixing until combined. Knead two to three times on a floured board.

3. Pat or roll the dough to 3/4-inch thick. Cut out biscuits with a biscuit cutter or the rim of a glass dipped in flour.

4. Place biscuits on a greased cookie sheet and bake at 425°F for about 12 minutes. Makes 14 biscuits.

Gingerbread Cookies

Use any leftover dough from your gingerbread house (see following pages) to make gingerbread cookies! Roll out the dough to 1/8-inch thick. Then let children cut out cookies using gingerbread boy and girl cookie cutters. You might also use Santa, reindeer, and tree-shaped cutters. Place the cookies on a greased cookie sheet and bake at 350°F for 10-15 minutes.

Book Nook

Catch a gingerbread story or learn more about gingerbread houses!

Gingerbread Baby by Jan Brett (Putnam, 1999)

The Gingerbread Doll by Susan Tewes (Houghton Mifflin, 2001)

Gingerbread Houses for Kids by Jennifer A. Ericsson (White Birch Press, 1998)

The Gingerbread Man by Jim Aylesworth (Scholastic, 1998)

Maisy Makes Gingerbread by Lucy Cousins (Candlewick, 1999)

Theme Houses

What kind of gingerbread house will you build? Here are a few fun themes to try:

* a witch's house (as in Hansel and Gretel), laden with cookies and candies
* a school house, decorated with gingerbread cookie numbers and ABC's
* a city apartment house
* a cozy cottage with marshmallow snowmen and a tin-foil pond in front

Winter Wonder

I grew up next to a nine hole golf course—and a wake-up call of "FOOOORE!" at 6 a.m. every spring, summer, and fall weekend of my childhood. To this day I have an aversion to golf and a love of winter! Only in winter did I have the luxury of sleeping late on the weekends. It was also the only time that the golf course wasn't off limits to my siblings and me.

We claimed the frozen rolling hills as our own personal playground from the first snowfall until the warm spring thaw. We entertained ourselves sleigh riding, skiing, and building igloos and snow forts all winter long. My brother and I made snow slushes with maple syrup purloined from the kitchen and traded them to our younger siblings and friends in exchange for favors. We had ongoing snowball rolling contests, as well as never-ending games of Fox and Geese played in twelve inches of snow with neighborhood friends long into dusk.

Though we had no television, computer, or video games, boredom was seldom a factor for us. Mother Nature provided us with the best toys imaginable. This fact, combined with my parents' awareness that we needed lots of exercise and fresh air, allowed us the freedom to spend much of our days outdoors, despite the cold New York winters.

This kind of creative outdoor free play is harder to give our children today. It's a sad fact that it is much more difficult to find safe places to play. Many of our children are spending more time in structured activities at a much younger age. Two-, three-, and four-year-olds are enrolled in everything from gymnastics, martial arts, dance, music, art, and computer lessons as well as soccer, t-ball, tennis, and yes, even golf instruction!

Brave the Elements

We can still provide children with outdoor play and the chance to discover the joys of winter; we just have to be a bit more creative and determined to get them outdoors every day. A few tips:

Help children dress for the cold weather. With waterproof gloves and mittens, Velcro boots, and lightweight but warm parkas, hats, and ski masks, kids can stay warm without feeling like the Abominable Snowman! Stress the importance of bringing appropriate winter apparel each morning. Plan to go outside during the warmest part of the day and play in the sun if possible.

Keep everyone toasty when they're outside by having a few active games in mind. Running games such as Fox and Geese, Can't Catch Me, or a rousing game of Simon Says are fun for getting preschoolers' blood pumping. Making snow angels, building snowmen and forts, and taking turns stomping out "Follow the Leader" paths will keep everyone warm even when the temperature hovers near freezing. Do keep your outdoor visits short, however, on excessively cold or windy days. On the days when it is freezing or below, have some outdoor fun inside by filling your water table or sink with snow!

Winter Wonderland

To a child, snow is like magic falling to the ground! Snowflakes are cold and wet and silent. Snow is for digging, building, rolling, and sliding. If you've been hibernating, now's the time to pile on layers of warm clothing and go out to explore! If you live in an area where it doesn't snow, you can still help children explore the concept of seasonal change: many of these activities do not require snow or even cold weather.

Winter Walk

Brrr! Winter is here and there's lots to talk about: *How has the weather changed? What has happened to the grass and ponds and lakes? Does the sky look different? What do you do for fun in the winter? How do animals keep warm? How does their fur change? How about their homes? Where are all the chipmunks, moles, and groundhogs? Where do you think the birds have gone?*

If you live in an area where there is snow, ask children, *What is snow? Where does snow come from? What makes it melt? What do you like or not like about playing in the snow?*

Bundle up and take a winter walk to see firsthand the changes the cold has brought. On your walk, play a game of "I Spy." Explain that a sign of winter can be a bare branch, a bird with its feathers fluffed out, an icicle, a frozen puddle, and, of course, snow! Whenever children see a sign of winter, they can call out "I spy winter!" Bring along a magnifying glass so children can look at some of their finds close up. It's especially fun to examine snowflakes!

Ice Castles

You don't need a yard full of snow to build an ice castle! Collect a variety of containers of different shapes and sizes. Small and large yogurt containers, film canisters, and plastic soda bottles with the necks cut off work especially well. Fill the containers with water, add some food coloring, and freeze. Run the containers briefly under warm water to slide the ice out. Then let children have fun building ice castles in the water table (or outdoors, in warmer climates)!

Winter Painting

If you have a yard full of snow outside, gather large paint brushes, old feather dusters, spray bottles, plastic containers and water tinted with food coloring for an afternoon of creative outdoor play! Place the tinted water in plastic containers and in spray bottles and space children far enough apart so they each have their own "snowspace." Let children use the brushes, dusters, and spray bottles to explore snow as a new painting surface.

If you don't have any real snow gracing your yard, fill ice cube trays with water. Place the trays in a freezer and let freeze. Then sprinkle different colors of powdered tempera paint on paper, and let children use the ice cubes as paintbrushes to swish the colors around their papers.

How Cold Is It?

"**I**t's freezing!" is a common remark from young children. How cold does it have to be to be *really* freezing? (32°F and below) Try these ideas to build children's understanding of temperature.

❋ Take a child's temperature (or your own) with a safety thermometer. Explain that we all usually have the same body temperature, 98.6°F. Then compare it to the temperature in the classroom and the temperature outdoors.

❋ Help children pour juice into paper cups and place a craft stick in each cup. Then set the cups on a tray and cover them. Set the tray outside in the morning. If it's freezing out, children will have juice pops by noon. If not, bring the juice cups inside and either drink the juice, or put them in the freezer!

Chicken Soup With Rice

Share the Maurice Sendak classic *Chicken Soup With Rice* (HarperCollins, 1962), then make a pot of this satisfying comfort food.

* 2 tablespoons olive oil
* 1 small garlic clove, minced
* 1 cup each chopped onion, carrots, celery, cabbage
* 1 cup corn (optional)
* 1 cup chopped green beans (optional)
* 3 quarts chicken stock (you can simply add chicken or vegetable bouillon cubes to the water)
* 2 cups chopped, cooked chicken
* 1 cup brown rice, raw
* 1 tablespoon chopped fresh dill (or 1/2 teaspoons dried)
* 1 tablespoon chopped parsley

1. In a large pot, saute garlic and vegetables in oil for five minutes.

2. Add chicken stock and bring to a boil (supervise children closely). Reduce heat to simmer.

3. Add the chicken, rice, dill, and parsley to the pot and simmer 45 minutes, until rice and vegetables are fully cooked. Season with salt and pepper. Serves 16 children.

Tip: If you cut the vegetables into strips first, children will be able to cut them into small pieces with plastic knives. Freeze an extra batch of soup and you'll have some on hand for that surprise snowstorm, or to soothe a case of the sniffles!

Thumb in the Thumbhole

Recite this version of a traditional verse with children. Chanting the poem will help children focus on the task at hand as they bundle up for the great outdoors.

Thumb in the thumbhole,
Fingers all together.
This is the poem
We say in mitten weather.

Bundle up your fingers,
Bundle up your toes,
And don't forget to wrap
A scarf around your nose!

—additional verse
by Annie Stiefel

Snow Dough

This white play dough has an icy, snowy texture.

The recipe calls for snow water (melted snow), but you can also use tap water. (If you are using snow water, make sure the snow you gather is clean.)

❄ 1 1/3 plus 1/2 cup snow water

❄ 2 cups kosher salt

❄ 1 cup cornstarch

1. Mix 1 1/3 cups of the snow water with salt and bring to a boil (supervise children closely). Simmer several minutes, stirring constantly. Remove from heat.

2. Mix the remaining snow water with the cornstarch and add to the salt water. Stir well, then let cool. Store snow dough in an airtight container.

3. For extra shine, have children work some silver glitter into the dough. Children can pound the dough flat and press out shapes with cookie cutters, or sculpt snow creatures. Dough will harden within 36 hours.

Cuddle up with these winter reads!

Copy Me, Copycub by Richard Edwards (HarperCollins, 1999)

Snow by Uri Shulevitz (Farrar Straus & Giroux, 1998)

Snowballs by Lois Ehlert (Harcourt, 2001)

The Snowman by Raymond Briggs (Random House, 1978)

Snow, Snow, Snow: Winter Poems for Children by Jane Yolen (Boyds Mills, 1998)

The Snowy Day by Ezra Jack Keats (Viking, 1962)

When It Starts to Snow by Phillis Gershator (Holt, 1998)

Icy Sun Catchers

Take a nature walk and collect pinecones, pine needles, pebbles, and so on. Back inside, let children place their treasures in aluminum pie pans. Then fill the pans with water and add food coloring in colors of your choice. Next, make the "hangers" by tying loops of string to small craft sticks. Place a stick in each pie pan with the string hanging over the edge, and then put the pie pans in the freezer (or outside, if the temperature is below 32°F). When frozen, unmold and hang from trees.

It's fun to see how long these icy sun catchers last. Hang one in the sun and one in the shade, and ask children which one they think will melt first. (If it's freezing out, point out that they will last until the temperature rises!)

Let's Sing!

Most young children love to sing and be sung to. Singing creates a sense of classroom community and builds confidence, as well as children's musical abilities. Children are also a wonderfully enthusiastic and nonjudgmental audience, so don't worry if you sing off-key or miss a beat. As long as you're enjoying yourself, they'll want to join right in!

Twinkle, Twinkle!

Give a new sparkle to the familiar song "Twinkle, Twinkle, Little Star" by letting children be the stars! Children will enjoy hearing their name in the verse and shaking their twinkling star ring.

1. For each child, you will need large paper plates (heavy ones work best), six star stickers (or cut out star shapes from paper), three feet of silver garland (available in craft stores), string or yarn, blue paint, two or three silver bells, and glitter and glue.

2. Cut out the centers of the paper plates. Then have children paint the plate rims blue, stick on the stars, and add glitter. Help children wind the garlands around their plate rims. Then punch holes in the plates and tie on bells with string or yarn.

3. Let children shake their star rings high over their heads as they sing "Twinkle, Twinkle, Little Star." Substitute a child's name for the word *star* and the phrase *how you are* for the phrase *what you are*. As children take turns being the star, have them hold their star rings in front of them to frame their faces. Or, have all children hold their rings to frame their faces as they sing!

Big Red Box

Teach children the following song (to the tune of "Polly Wolly Doodle"):

Oh I wish I had a big red box,
To put that [child's name] in,
I'd put [him/her] in
and clap, clap, clap,
and take [him/her] out again.

Select a sturdy cardboard box (large enough to fit a child) and let children paint the box red. When dry, set it on its side, sing the song, and encourage children to clap along. Let each child have a turn climbing in and out of the box as you sing.

B-I-N-G-O

Practice this traditional song with children:

There was a farmer had a dog,
and Bingo was his name-o,
B-I-N-G-O, B-I-N-G-O, B-I-N-G-O,
and Bingo was his name-o.

To build letter identification skills, spell out the song on a flannel board with felt letters B, I, N, G, and O. Let children place the felt letters on the feltboard. Sing the song once through. Then sing the song again, this time removing the felt letter B, deleting it from the song, and clapping in its place. Repeat four more times, each time removing another letter. By the fifth round you will be clapping for each of the five letters.

After singing, you might cut out dog shapes from paper and let each child use bingo bottles (see below) to decorate their own dog.

Bingo Bottles

These irresistible art tools are a cross between markers and watercolors.

Bingo players use sponge-topped plastic bottles to mark their bingo cards, then discard the bottles when empty. Ask a local bingo hall to save empty bottles for you. Remove the top of each bottle, fill halfway with water, and then add enough food coloring to give the water an intense hue. Replace the lid and close tightly. Children can press the sponge-top onto a piece of paper to make a big colorful dot!

The More We Get Together

Teach children a friendship song they can act out with their classmates—in two languages!

(To the tune of "Did You Ever See a Lassie?")

The more we get together, together, together,
The more we get together, the happier we'll be.
*(form a circle, hold hands, swing arms,
clap on the word "happier")*
For your friends are my friends,
And my friends are your friends.
(point to yourself and your friends)
The more we get together, the happier we'll be.
(hold hands, swing, and clap again)

Lo mas que nos reunimos, reunimos, reunimos,
Lo mas que nos reunimos, seremos felices.
Tu amigos son mis amigos,
Y mis amigos son tus amigos.
Lo mas que nos reunimos, seremos felices.

After singing, make a friendship wreath. Trace children's hands on lightweight cardboard and cut them out. Have children paint the hands and then staple them together to form a circle. Attach a ribbon and hang on the door.

Book Nook

Sing along to a good story!

Baby Beluga by Raffi (Crown, 1997)

How Much Is that Doggie in the Window? by Iza Trapani (Charlesbridge, 2004)

Hush Little Baby by Sylvia Long (Chronicle, 1997)

If You're Happy and You Know It by Nicki Weiss (Greenwillow, 1987)

I'm a Little Teapot by Iza Trapani (Charlesbridge, 1999)

Shake My Sillies Out by Raffi (Crown, 1988)

Skip to My Lou by Nadine Bernard Westcott (Little Brown, 2000)

Songs from Mother Goose by Nancy Larrick (Harper & Row, 1989)

Twinkle, Twinkle Little Star by Julia Noonan (Scholastic, 1992)

Start the New Year Singing!

✳ Use a song to soothe a child who is having a hard day, to get a group hopping on a rainy morning, or to ease transitions from one activity to another.

✳ Start a music lending library with family members or other teachers or caregivers.

✳ See if there are any parents in the group who play an instrument, and invite them in for a special music session.

✳ Each week, choose a child to be "songleader."

Color Fun

Color surrounds us every day, and young children are discovering its infinite variety. They enjoy working with crayons, chalk, markers, and paint, and take pride in being able to identify and name the colors around them. Exploring color in the classroom provides the perfect opportunity to introduce new vocabulary; in addition to color names, there are words such as *shade*, *tint*, *dull*, and *bright*. As you bring attention to the multitude of colors in our world, point out color variations as well: *How many different shades of green can you see out our window?*

The Color Game

Invite a volunteer to choose a color and call it out, for example: *Bring me red.* The group then looks for small, easy to carry, red objects and puts them in the center of the room. Invite children to examine the objects and point out their different shades. Then have the next child name a new color to gather. You can also turn this into a great clean-up game: *Let's put away everything blue!*

Let the Sun Shine

Long ago, people made dyes out of fruits, vegetables, and flowers. Children today can turn natural onion skins into a thing of beauty: the color yellow! Display these in windows so the sun shines through.

1. Have children help collect discarded onion skins from home (you will need a total of four cups). Each child needs a six-inch square of white cotton fabric. Write children's names on the squares using a waterproof marker.

2. Dampen the cloth squares slightly and wring out any excess water. Then let children place a marble or small rock in the center of each cloth square. Help them twist one or two rubber bands around the cloth very tightly to hold the marble or rock in place. Keep the cloth squares moist by placing them in a plastic bag.

3. Next, place all the onion skins in a pot, cover with two quarts of cold water, and simmer for about 30 minutes or until you have a strong yellow color. Remove the skins with tongs. Then add the damp cloth squares (with the marbles inside) to the yellow liquid, and bring to a boil (adult only). Simmer 30–60 minutes until the cloth is a rich yellow and let cool. Remove the cloth, allow it to dry, and remove the rubber bands. You've made yellow!

Color Windows

Children are often surprised to see that mixing two colors makes a new color. Here's a fun way to mix colors and give children a new view of the world around them.

1. To make one set of color windows, you will need three 6-inch by 8-inch Styrofoam produce trays, a 4- by 12-inch piece each of red, yellow, and blue cellophane, and masking tape.

2. Cut a 3- by 5-inch opening in the center of each tray.

3. Fold each piece of cellophane in half. Then place each piece flat on a tray and secure by taping the edges.

4. Let children take turns looking through a single color window. Then stack two color windows together and have children look through the new window. How many colors can they make from the three primary colors? Take your color windows outside and let children view the great outdoors through their new color windows!

Color Dance

Read *Color Dance* by Ann Jonas (Greenwillow, 1999) with children. Then have a color dance of your own!

Purchase 1/4 yard each of red, yellow, blue, orange, green, and purple polyester lining fabric. Cut into three-inch wide ribbons for children to dance with. (You can also use colorful crepe paper streamers, which are inexpensive, but less durable than fabric). Play music and let children dance, varying the selections from loud and boisterous to quiet and slow. You might take photographs of children's performance and display them!

Rainbow Fun

Rainbows are natural wonders perfect for your study of colors. Try these fun activities:

* R is for rainbow! Have children practice writing the letter R in markers and crayons, using rainbow colors.

* Read Lois Ehlert's *Planting a Rainbow* (Voyager, 1992)

* Have children tell about a time they saw a rainbow.

* Make big rainbow crayons! Melt pieces of old crayons (all colors) in muffin tins (lined with paper) on a 200°F oven.

* Make rainbows for snack! You'll want to do this over several days. Gather fast-setting gelatin mixes in red, orange, yellow, green, blue, and purple. Make the red gelatin and pour a small amount in the bottom of each clear glass (about one-sixth of the cup). Let set. Repeat with each color in rainbow order (red, orange, yellow, green, blue, purple). Add a whipped cream cloud on top!

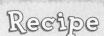

Recipe

Rainbow Dough

Very young children love to pound and squeeze this soft, oily play dough. It's also great for moisturizing winter-dry hands!

Mix together three cups flour, 1/2 cup oil, and 1/2 cup plus three tablespoons of water. Divide dough evenly among children and let them each add two drops of their favorite color food coloring. They'll enjoy watching the color spread through the dough as they work it in with their hands. Then invite children to pair off and knead different-colored pieces of dough together.

Exploring Colors

Create a color-exploration center in the classroom. Gather boxes of crayons and chalk and place them in the art center along with paint, easels, and smocks. Encourage children to experiment with the different media, create new colors, and give their new colors names.

What colors might we find outdoors this time of year? Go on a color walk with children to find out. Bring paper and pencil and list all the colors they find.

Wet Chalk Rainbow

Dip chalk in yogurt! The yogurt makes the chalk colors more brilliant, and acts as a fixative to keep the chalk from smearing when it dries.

1. Cut a large rainbow shape from white butcher paper.

2. Mix 1/2 cup plain yogurt with 2 tablespoons of water and show children how to dip colored chalk into the yogurt. Remind them not to taste the yogurt!

3. Color the rainbow together: red, orange, yellow, green, blue, indigo, and violet. Introduce new color vocabulary by pointing out *indigo*.

Book Nook

Enjoy a rainbow of books at story time!

Brown Bear, Brown Bear, What Do You See? by Bill Martin, Jr. (Holt, 1992)

The Color Kittens by Margaret Wise Brown (Golden, 2001)

Colors: A First Discovery Book by Pascale De Bourgoing (Scholastic, 1989)

Is It Red? Is It Yellow? Is It Blue? by Tana Hoban (Greenwillow, 1987)

Mouse Paint by Ellen Stoll Walsh (Harcourt, 1989)

White Rabbit's Color Book by Alan Baker (Kingfisher, 1994)

Who Said Red? by Mary Serfozo (McElderry, 1988)

Dinosaur Days

Dinosaurs may be extinct, but children's fascination with these incredible creatures is very much alive! Paleontologists have made discoveries about dinosaurs by studying fossils of their skeletons, tracks, and eggs. In this theme, children will have fun learning about dinosaurs—and making discoveries of their own.

Dino Eggs

Children may be surprised to learn that dinosaurs hatched from eggs, just like birds! Children can hatch some dinosaur eggs of their own.

1. Mix one cup flour with one cup water. Add four cups boiling water. Simmer for three minutes, then cool.

2. Have children tear newspaper strips about one inch wide.

3. Blow up a balloon for each child and tape a small plastic dinosaur onto its surface.

4. Have children dip the paper in the flour mixture and wrap around the balloon. Let dry overnight then repeat the next day. Hanging the knotted part of the balloon on a clothesline (with a clothespin) works well.

5. Have children paint their eggs. Let dry. Help the baby dinosaur "hatch" by poking a hole (large enough for the dinosaur to fit through) with a pencil and popping the balloon.

I'm a Dinosaur

(To the tune of "I'm a Little Tea Pot")

I'm a Diplodocus,
Eating evergreens.
I'm long and I'm tall,
But I'm not really mean.
I only use my whiptail
When I have to fight,
If I see a meat eater
Coming into sight!

I'm an Allosaurus,
Strong and stout.
Here are my teeth,
Here is my snout.
When I'm really hungry,
Hear me shout:
"I'll eat you up
If you don't watch out!"

—Annie Stiefel
& Jean Stiefel

Dino Dough

Children can use this all-purpose play dough to create dinosaur bones for a pretend dig. Explain that paleontologists gather their information by studying fossils found on digs. Let children go on a dig right in your classroom or backyard (just bury bones in the sand table)!

* 1 cup salt
* 2 cups flour
* 2 teaspoons cream of tartar
* 2 cups water
* 2 tablespoons vegetable oil

1. Mix all ingredients in a pot and cook over medium heat, stirring until the dough begins to thicken and form a ball.

2. Then remove the dough from the pot and allow it to cool slightly.

3. Divide the dough into balls and add a different color food coloring to each ball. Children can form into bone shapes.

4. Bake at 200°F for two to three hours.

Dino Facts

Ask children to speculate about dinosaurs. Then do research in library books to check children's understanding.

* What do you think happened to all the dinosaurs?
* How big were the biggest dinosaurs?
* How small were the smallest dinosaurs?
* Could some dinosaurs fly?
* What does extinct *mean?*
* What is a fossil?
* What is a paleontologist?
* What colors were the dinosaurs?
* What kinds of sounds did they make?

Dinos All Day Long

Infuse your day with dinosaurs! Here are some great ways to integrate the theme into your everyday routines.

✳ Enrich the dramatic play center with toy dinosaurs, dinosaur puppets, child-made eggs and bones (see pages 80 and 81), shovels, plastic plants, magnifying glasses, a blanket for a cave, and books about dinosaurs.

✳ Have children practice the letter Dd at the writing center.

✳ At the science center, provide "stone dough" (mix and knead together 1/2 cup of salt, one cup flour, 1/2 cup cold brewed coffee and one cup used coffee grounds) and objects for fossil prints, such as twigs, seashells, coins, and thick leaves. Children can take and flatten a handful of dough and press an item into it to make a fossil. Dry overnight.

Here are some great reads for junior paleontologists!

The Big Book of Dinosaurs: A First Book for Young Children by Angela Wilkes (DK, 1994)

Bones, Bones, Dinosaur Bones by Byron Barton (Crowell, 1990)

Danny and the Dinosaur by Syd Hoff (HarperCollins, 1993)

Digging Up Dinosaurs by Aliki (HarperCollins, 1988)

Dinosaur Cousins? by Bernard Most (Harcourt, 1987)

Dinosaur Roar! by Paul & Henrietta Strickland (Puffin, 2002)

How Big Were the Dinosaurs? by Bernard Most (Harcourt, 1994)

How Do Dinosaurs Say Goodnight? by Jane Yolen (Scholastic, 2000)

If the Dinosaurs Came Back by Bernard Most (Harcourt, 1991)

My Visit to the Dinosaurs by Aliki (Crowell, 1985)

Saturday Night at the Dinosaur Stomp by Carol Diggory Shields (Candlewick, 2002)

Kids in the Kitchen

In many parts of the country, February is a great time to stay inside and cook! In this month, as in the other months in the *Almanac*, you'll find several recipes perfect for little hands. Cooking provides great satisfaction for young children and is a wonderful way to give kids the attention, independence, and accomplishments they crave. It's real work, just like adults do! They can't iron or drive yet, but they can cook. Cooking is a natural way to incorporate many age-appropriate skills into your program, such as:

* Math skills, as children measure, count, weigh, divide, estimate, and keep track of time

* Science concepts, as they learn about the chemistry of food and how it changes during the cooking process

* Language and reading readiness, as they describe foods, flavors, textures, and processes

* Logical thinking, as they learn to follow recipe sequences

* Social studies concepts, as they learn about the world around them through food from other cultures

* Motor skills and hand-eye coordination, as children cut, mash, mix, pour, pinch, punch, scoop, spill, sponge, sweep, and stir

* Social skills, as they cooperate and help one another to achieve a goal

Recipe for Success

Here are some pointers to maximize success in the kitchen.

* Always have children wash hands before beginning and remind them to keep hands away from their faces as they work.

* Remind children to ask before they taste (raw eggs in batters and doughs are a particular concern).

* Teach your kids a code word to warn them when you'll be opening the oven, taking hot water off the stove, and so on. I simply say "hot stuff!" and then make sure they're out of harm's way.

* Remember to start simply with recipes of just a few ingredients and several basic processes. Whatever recipe you're using should be one that you have made successfully before. Make sure you have all the ingredients before you start.

* Allow plenty of time. My rule of thumb is to double the time it might take an adult to prepare a recipe. Also, pick a time of day when your kids are alert.

* Encourage participation and fun, rather than perfection.

* Have alternative activities for those who don't want to participate or who have short attention spans. Be creative and flexible with kids in the kitchen.

I Am Special

It's wonderful to watch children form their own identities as they become aware of who they are, what they can do, and how they fit in to the larger world of friends and family. In this popular theme, you'll focus on children's unique qualities and capabilities with activities that highlight and celebrate their accomplishments. Children grow more confident in their abilities as they become aware of their many successes, no matter how small. So. . . make children feel special by giving them the chance to say "I can do it all by myself!"

My Name

Write each child's name in permanent marker on a large index card and attach a magnetic strip to the back.

Place all the cards in a basket. Tell children that there is something special for each of them in the basket, and invite them to find it. Help children recognize the spellings of their names.

When children have found their names, have them trace over the letters in their names with glue. Provide a variety of collage materials, such as dried beans, glitter, colored sand, confetti, and dyed rice and pasta. Let children select the materials they like and sprinkle them over the glue. Let dry and have children take them home to display on their refrigerators.

Paper Bag Vests

Boost self-esteem with these personalized paper bag vests.

Gather a paper grocery bag for each child. Slit the bag up the middle and cut out armholes and a neck hole. If there is printing on the bag, turn it inside out.

To personalize children's vests, help children write their names or initials on the bag. Have children add self-portraits, as well as drawings or photographs of family members, friends, and pets. Children can also attach magazine pictures of favorite toys, books, foods, and animals. You might even invite children to dictate a joke, riddle, special memory, or accomplishment to write on the vest. Add handprints, fingerprints, and personal facts such as age and height. Provide children with collage materials to glue on their vests, such as buttons, beads, ribbon, foil and fabric scraps, and glitter.

"I Can" Cans

Making an "I Can" can is a fun way to encourage and applaud new accomplishments.

1. Discuss with children all the things they can do. Write down their ideas on slips of paper along with their names and the date (for instance, *I can button my own shirt. Nick, February, 2004).*

2. Each child will need a photograph of him or herself and a coffee can with a plastic lid. Write the phrase *I Can* on index cards, along with each child's name. Then let children decorate their cards using pencils, crayons, or markers and tape the cards onto the cans.

3. Have children paint their cans with thick glue, such as Mod Podge (available at craft stores). While wet, attach the photo and coat with two more layers of Modge Podge. Children may also like to add scraps of paper to decorate their cans.

4. Cut a slot in each plastic lid and put children's "accomplishment slips" into the cans. Help children add to their "I Can" cans every week, and share what's inside periodically at circle time.

Recipe

Bread Sculpture

Children love creating freeform dough sculptures.

❋ 1/2 cup salt

❋ 3/4 cup hot water

❋ 1 tablespoon vegetable oil

❋ 2 cups whole wheat flour

Mix salt and water until salt is dissolved (supervise closely for safety). Add oil and flour and mix thoroughly. Makes two cups.

You can use this mixture to make keepsake handprints. Simply roll and flatten the dough into circles of about 1/3-inch thick. Let each child press his or her hand into a circle to make an impression. Dry the handprint in a 150°F oven for one to two hours, turning once. Invite children to paint their handprints or sculptures with tempera paints, let dry, and take home as a special gift.

Book Nook

Celebrate children's individuality with these special books.

All About You by Catherine Anholt (Viking, 1992)

Chester's Way by Kevin Henkes (Greenwillow, 1988)

Feelings by Aliki (Greenwillow, 1984)

I Like Being Me: Poems by Judy Lalli (Free Spirit, 1997)

I Like Me by Nancy Carlson (Viking, 1988)

I Like to Be Little by Charlotte Zolotow (Crowell, 1987)

People by Peter Spier (Doubleday, 1980)

We Are All Alike…We Are All Different by the Cheltenham Elementary School Kindergartners (Scholastic, 2002)

You Are Special

Boost children's confidence and self-esteem by using their names as you verbalize positive behavior and special qualities. This is as simple as saying "Zoë knows how to share her toys" or "Zach, you really enjoy spending time at the writing table." It's a surefire way to make each child in your classroom feel special!

Our Special Book

Create a scrapbook filled with classroom memories.

1. Use lightweight cardboard or posterboard for pages. Punch three holes in the sides of pages and bind with two-inch rings (available at office supply stores).

2. Encourage children to find mementos of the things they've done each week to glue or tape into their scrapbook. The memento might be a drawing, a pretty leaf they collected, an apple print, a photograph of a group project or trip, or even a dictated recollection of a favorite activity. Remember to date each entry and label them with children's names. Add to your scrapbook every week, and share your growing book of memories with children at circle time.

3. As you build your scrapbook, let each child have a turn taking the album home to share with family and friends. This is a great way to make families feel included, and help children see how they've changed and grown throughout the year.

Special Reminders

There are lots of ways to make each and every child feel special.

❋ Designate a cubby for each child so he or she has private space.

❋ Have hand mirrors available in the dramatic play center, and shatterproof full-length mirrors mounted at children's eye-level.

❋ Occasionally tape-record children speaking, reading or singing and play it back for them.

❋ Regularly ask children for their input, such as *What story shall we read today, Jamie?*

"I Can" Hourglass

What can children do in a short period of time? Make a sand timer to find out!

Before children arrive, use two clean baby food jars with lids, and 1/4 cup of fine sand (available in craft stores). Hot glue the two lids together. With a large nail, hammer a hole through the center of each lid. Then pour the sand into one baby food jar, run a bead of hot glue around the tops of the jars, and screw on the lids. Put masking tape around the lids to complete the timer.

When children arrive, show them the timer and let them have fun trying to wash their hands, do a puzzle, or pick up toys before the sand runs out. Children also enjoy simply shaking the timer and watching the sand form a mountain as it flows from one side to the other.

Friendship

Playing together, sharing, and taking turns are important skills for preschoolers to practice every day. By watching and listening to children interact, intervening at appropriate times, and modeling good social behaviors, you'll help children build the skills they need for healthy friendships. Just in time for Valentine's Day, this theme is filled with activities that celebrate and encourage friendship, cooperation, sharing, and caring.

Friendly Hands

Children and family members work together to create this friendship poster.

Cut a large heart from heavy paper or tagboard. Make three ink pads by folding dampened paper towels in half and spreading them with pink, lavender, and red paint. At morning drop-off or afternoon pick-up time, let children and family members choose colors, press their palms into the color, and then onto the paper heart. Invite everyone to write their name under the handprints. Display your poster to celebrate the friendships in your classroom community.

Rainbow Pasta & Rice

Dry pasta is a great material for art projects. To create colored pasta, mix one cup of rubbing alcohol with one tablespoon of food coloring. Add a quarter-pound of uncooked pasta and soak for one hour, stirring often. Drain and dry pasta on paper towels.

For brightly colored rice (perfect for collages and sand tables), mix one cup of uncooked rice with 1/4 cup water, add food coloring, and stir. Let soak for 30 minutes. Drain and spread rice on a baking sheet to dry.

Friends Album

Build literacy and social skills at the same time.

1. Create a blank book by punching holes down the left edges of light-colored construction paper (use enough sheets for each child to have one side). Use heavier paper for the front and back covers, and lace the pages together with yarn. Have each child write his or her name on the cover of the album to create a name collage.

2. Designate one page of the album for each child in the group and title it *Our Friend (child's name)*. Tape a picture of the child to the center of the page and let children dictate reasons this child is special to them, or describe activities they like to do together, such as *I like to do puzzles with James.*

3. Add new photos as children join your group, and new quotes as their friendships grow and change. Share the book with children at circle time or story time.

Friendship Necklaces

Celebrate friendships in the classroom with special necklaces.

Give each child a length of string and a selection of dyed ziti pasta (see left). Let children thread the ziti and beads onto the string. Encourage them to create patterns such as red, blue, red, blue. Invite children to trade necklaces with a friend.

Recipe

Valentine Lolli-Cookies

Make a batch of lollipop cookies with children. If you double the recipe, you'll have enough to send home as Valentine gifts.

* 1/2 cup vegetable shortening
* 1/2 cup butter
* 2/3 cup white sugar
* 2/3 cup brown sugar
* 2 eggs
* 2 teaspoons vanilla extract
* 2 cups white flour
* 1 1/2 cups whole wheat flour
* 2 teaspoons baking powder
* 1 teaspoon salt
* 4 teaspoons pumpkin pie spice (or 1 teaspoon each of cinnamon, nutmeg, ginger, and allspice)
* 24 craft sticks

1. Mix shortening, butter, and sugar together until light and fluffy.

2. Add eggs and vanilla and stir.

3. Add flour, baking powder, salt, and spices. Cover and refrigerate for one to two hours.

4. Roll the dough out to 1/3-inch thick and use heart-shaped cookie cutters to make Valentine cookies. Transfer the cookies to an ungreased baking sheet with a spatula and insert a craft stick 1 1/2 inches into the base of each cookie.

5. Bake at 375°F for 10 minutes, until light brown. Makes 24 three-inch cookies. (If you'd like a hard, glossy finish, have children paint their baked cookies with sweetened condensed milk tinted with red food coloring.)

Cookies to Share

Teach this fingerplay to children as you bake your Valentine cookies.

Cookies to share,
One, two, three.
(*hold up three fingers, one at a time*)

One for you,
(*point to a friend*)

And two for me.
(*point to self*)

Oh, no, no, no,
(*shake head and finger*)

That won't do!
Let's break the extra one in two!
(*pantomime breaking and sharing cookie*)

—Annie Stiefel

Book Nook

Books are for sharing! Here are a few friendship books to try.

Corduroy by Don Freeman (Viking, 1968)

For Pete's Sake by Ellen Stoll Walsh (Harcourt, 1998)

Frog and Toad Are Friends by Arnold Lobel (Harper & Row, 1970)

George and Martha by James Marshall (Houghton, 1974)

How to Be a Friend by Laurene Krasny Brown & Marc Brown (Little Brown, 1998)

Jessica by Kevin Henkes (Greenwillow, 1989)

Making Friends by Fred Rogers
(Putnam, 1996)

Otis by Janie Bynum (Harcourt, 2000)

More Friendly Fun

Celebrate friendship and Valentine's Day with these quick and easy ideas.

✳ Talk about friendship with children. *What is a friend? What do you like to do with your friends inside and outside of school?*

✳ Invite children to bring in a toy from home to share with friends in the classroom.

✳ Make heart puzzles. Cut cardboard hearts in half, each one with a different zig-zag or curved cut. Give each child a half. Can children find the partner with the matching piece?

✳ For sweet-smelling Valentines, drizzle glue onto a paper heart. Then sprinkle it with strawberry or cherry gelatin powder.

✳ Talk about hearts with children. Ask: *Where is your heart? What does it do? How do you keep it healthy?* Invite children to feel their heartbeat with their hands, both at rest and after exercising.

Terrific Teeth

Children are naturally curious about their bodies, and teeth hold a special fascination. February is National Children's Dental Health Month—a great time to help children establish healthy dental habits. Why not plan a trip to a dentist's office for a tour? Even if you are not able to make a personal visit, many dentists will be happy to supply each child with a goodie bag, complete with toothbrush, floss, stickers, and pamphlets.

Healthy Habits Tooth Brushing Chart

Involve family members in helping children start healthy dental habits with this incentive chart.

To make the charts, cut out a large toothbrush shape for each child from cardboard. Let children decorate it with paint, markers, or crayons. Make photocopies of the current month's calendar page and staple or tape it to the cardboard toothbrush. Then punch holes in each end of the toothbrush and use dental floss as string, tying an end through each hole to create a hanger.

Children can hang their charts on their bedroom bulletin board or door, or in the bathroom. Parents and caregivers can reward children with a check mark or sticker each morning and evening they brush. You might supply the initial set of stickers, so families can get started right away. You can also provide copies of calendar pages for use in upcoming months.

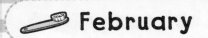

Brush, Brush, Brush!

Have children pantomime brushing their teeth as they sing this song!

(To the tune of "Row, Row, Row, Your Boat")

Brush, brush, brush our teeth,
Brush them pearly white.
Keep away the cavities,
Morning, noon and night!

Brush, brush, brush our teeth,
Use water and toothpaste.
'Round and 'round,
Both up and down,
What a sparkly taste!

Rinse, rinse, rinse with water,
Wash it down the drain.
Rinse all clean and now you know
How to play the toothbrush game!

—*Annie Stiefel*

Brush Those Teeth

Create a smile that children can really scrub! Each child will need five small white ceramic floor tiles (these are inexpensive and available at tile stores), a clean Styrofoam produce tray, and an old, sterilized toothbrush.

Using a permanent marker, draw two eyes and a nose on the tray. Then glue on the white tiles in the shape of a smile. When the faces are finished, let children use a write-on/wipe-off marker to put "plaque" on the teeth. Then have them brush the teeth shiny clean with a dry toothbrush!

Stain a Tooth

Demonstrate the importance of regular tooth-brushing with this simple experiment.

1. Prepare four white hard-boiled eggs to represent teeth.

2. Let children gently tap the eggs and then tap their own teeth with their fingers. Explain that both the shell on the egg and the enamel on their teeth are porous, which means they have tiny openings. Even though we can't see them, the openings are big enough to let liquids come through, so some drinks can stain our teeth if we don't brush well.

3. Place one egg in a glass of water, one in a glass of cola, one in red punch drink, and one in tea or coffee.

4. Record children's guesses as to what will happen to each egg. What color will the eggs turn?

5. Leave the eggs in the glasses for three days, checking daily for changes in the shell. Then peel the eggs to see if some of the color has seeped through to stain the egg whites.

Sink your teeth into a good book!

Arthur's Tooth by Marc Brown (Little Brown, 1987)

Dr. DeSoto by William Steig (Farrar Straus & Giroux, 1982)

Going to the Dentist by Fred Rogers (Putnam, 1989)

How Many Teeth? by Paul Showers (HarperCollins, 1991)

Rosie's Baby Tooth by Maryann McDonald (Atheneum, 1991)

Throw Your Tooth on the Roof: Tooth Traditions from Around the World by Selby B. Beeler (Houghton Mifflin, 1998)

Tooth Fairy Math Manipulatives

Tear foam "peanuts" in half to represent teeth and place at the math center. Include a bowl of loose change and invite children to play tooth fairy! Children assign each tooth a value and then do the math (for instance, if each tooth is worth a penny, how much would the tooth fairy leave for ten teeth?) You might also place these at the dramatic play center.

Carrot Slaw

Here's a simple recipe that's full of vitamins and calcium for growing teeth. To make six servings, combine the following and mix well:

* 1/2 cup currants or raisins
* 1 cup vanilla yogurt
* 6 carrots

Shred the carrots in a food processor (adult only), or use a peeler. You might teach children to peel a carrot by holding it at the top in one hand and holding the peeler in the other hand, peeling downward in long strokes. Be sure to supervise closely for safety. Try substituting peach or lemon yogurt for vanilla to give the slaw a different taste!

Amazing Apples

Explain that because of their crunchy texture, apples help us keep our teeth clean! (carrots and celery do, too). After lunch, ask *What do your teeth feel like right now?* Then give each child an apple and invite them to take a few bites. *What do your teeth feel like now? How do they feel different?*

Toothbrush Paintbrushes

Ask families to donate their worn-out toothbrushes to use as paintbrushes.

To sterilize, soak the toothbrushes in bleach, then rinse well. Then cut out a large paper toothbrush shape for each child. Using the toothbrushes as painting tools, children can decorate their toothbrushes with tempera paints. If you add a squirt of glue to the paint, children can finish off their creations with a sprinkle of glitter.

Tooth Talk

Here are a few discussion-starters.

* *What do we use our teeth for?* (biting, chewing, talking, and smiling)
* *How many teeth do you have?*
* *Do you use certain teeth for certain things?* (chewing with molars, tearing with canines)
* *How many of your teeth are pointy? How many are flat?*

Puppet Play

Puppets have natural appeal to children, and Sergei Prokofiev's musical setting for the story "Peter and the Wolf" has been a favorite for generations. You can combine the two for a lively exploration of puppets, music, crafts, and dramatic play. Introduce young children to "Peter and the Wolf" by reading one of the many illustrated versions (see page 99). Then borrow a recording of the Prokofiev score from the library and play it throughout the week, pointing out the different characters' musical themes as children listen.

Put on a Show

Invite children to help you make each of the characters for the play (see pages 96–98). When the puppets are complete, help children work together to put on a show of *Peter and the Wolf.* You can invite family members and friends, and you might even make your own puppet theater for the performance (see page 99). Play the musical score as children put on their shows!

Peter

For a Peter puppet, you will need a three to four-inch foam egg (available at craft stores). Insert a craft stick into the smaller end of the egg. Then create Peter's face with fabric scraps, yarn, beads, buttons, and markers. Twist a pipe cleaner around the craft stick to represent arms, and secure it with glue. A strip of fabric can make a warm scarf, a small coil of string hung on one arm can represent Peter's rope, and folded paper can make a hat.

The Bird

To make a bird puppet, you will need a small paper cup, colored paper, a craft stick, and small colorful feathers (available at craft stores). Cut an orange paper triangle beak for each puppet, and punch out some black circles for eyes using a hole punch. Have children glue the beak, eyes, and feathers to the cup. Then tape a craft stick inside the cup for a handle.

The Duck

For the duck puppet, cut out a duck shape from lightweight cardboard. Let children color the duck with markers or crayons. When they are finished, cut two holes at the bottom of the duck and invite a child to poke his or her fingers through the holes to represent the duck's legs. Show them how to move their fingers to make their duck waddle!

The Cat

Paint the backs of two paper plates with watercolors. When dry, attach a paper towel tube to one plate using rubber cement. Then sandwich the tube between the two plates by gluing or stapling the second plate to the first. Use triangles of felt or paper for the cat's ears, eyes, and nose. Silver or gold stars make great pupils for the cat's eyes. Use pipe cleaners for whiskers. For a tail that really swishes, glue on a 12-inch section of chenille bumps (available at craft stores).

The Grandfather

Use a paper lunch bag (flat side up) to represent Peter's grandfather's face. Create hair and facial features using markers, crayons, bits of felt, and yarn. When dry, stuff the bag half full with crumpled newspaper. Then insert a wooden spoon, paint stirrer, or tongue depressor and gather the bag closed. Twist a pipe cleaner around the bag tightly and bend the ends, creating arms. Children can glue on cotton balls for a beard, and decorate a small plastic bowl for a hat.

The Wolf

To make the wolf, place a small sock on your hand, pushing your fingers all the way to the toe. Show children how a sock puppet can "talk". To create the wolf's mouth, cut a 1 1/2-inch square from pink or red contact paper. Crease it once diagonally across the middle, folding the square from point to point. Then peel off the backing. Have the child wearing the sock puppet open his or her hand while you attach the mouth with the crease horizontally at the back.

Create ears, eyes, nose, teeth, tongue, and tail by gluing on fabric and paper scraps, buttons, beads, chenille bumps, and yarn.

Puppet Tips

* For a puppet theater, remove the bottom of a large appliance box and slit the box open along one corner edge so that the box can be laid out flat. Cut out a window on one side, and let children help paint the box. When dry, stand the box up like a folding screen, taping the top flaps together for support. Then let the show go on!

* When making puppets, remember to keep the focus on process rather than product. Children's puppets will all come out differently. Encourage their individuality and let their imaginations soar.

* Look in thrift shops and yard sales to add to your puppet collection. For an excellent wholesale source, call Folkmanis at 800-654-8922.

* For more puppet-making ideas, try *Simple Puppets from Everyday Materials* by Barbara Buetter (Sterling, 1996).

Try different versions of *Peter and the Wolf*.

Erna Voigt's version of *Peter and the Wolf* (David Godine, 1990) is wonderful not only for the artist's detailed and colorful drawings, but also for the representative instruments from the musical score on each page. You might also look for these versions by the following illustrators:

Vagin Vladimir
(Scholastic, 2000)

Charles Mikolaycak
(Viking, 1986)

Peter Bailey
(Boosey & Hawkes, 2001)

Quick & Easy Puppets

It's simple to make puppets from all sorts of materials.

For bodies, try:

* Paper cups
* Socks
* Paper plates
* Paper bags
* Toilet paper tubes
* Empty, clear soda bottles or milk cartons cut in half

For features, use:

* Buttons
* Felt pieces
* Yarn
* Rick-rack
* Wiggly eyes
* Pipe cleaners
* Permanent marker
* Feathers

And . . .

* For finger puppets, cut off the tips of gloves.
* Use paper plates to create large faces.
* A large wooden spoon or spatula can become a face and body.
* Let children think up their own ways to make puppets. The possibilities are endless!

All Aboard the S.S. Imagination

While emptying closets recently in the home in which I grew up, I discovered a bit of my past—my childhood spaceship! Hunched in the dark, I could make out a few pencil drawings on the wall of gauges, buttons, and controls. Memories flooded back: trips to the moon, crash landings, radio signals, and Morse code tapped out on the bottom of a pot. These images were as familiar as if it were yesterday. I crawled out with a new appreciation for the power of imagination.

Imagination as a Tool

Imagination is an incredible resource that's available to us all our lives! Young children use their imaginations constantly as they grapple with new skills and concepts. Children use imagination as a stepping stone to explore new experiences and emotions, and to act out or try on adult roles. In the elementary years and throughout our lives, imagination shows itself in artwork, oral language, and creative writing.

We often ease ourselves into new situations by simply imagining them in advance (such as when athletes picture themselves crossing the finish line). Imagination can facilitate problem-solving and help us overcome obstacles. As teachers, it's important for us to support children's creative and imaginative nature and let them know how valuable it is. This takes enthusiasm, modeling, encouragement, empathy, and lots of creative thinking—and it's much easier if you're in touch with your own imaginative side first!

Set Sail

Take a look at your program's setting from a child's point of view. Imagination is fed through sensory experiences, so make sure the environment is rich with a wide variety of music, good literature, and interesting props.

It's also important to let children see you using your own imagination. Light a spark with image-provoking questions or pantomimes, and then watch the magic happen! For instance, one rainy morning I had several rather distracted children in my care. I lined up four chairs, sat in one, grabbed hold of an imaginary steering wheel, and in less than a minute, I had their attention. "What are you doing?" they asked. "I'm going fishing in my motor boat," I replied. "Want to come?" They hopped on, and then more children pulled up chairs so as not to miss the ride. We sang a verse of "Five Little Fishes" before I hopped off and asked a child if she'd like to take a turn driving. On that trip, Chris caught 25 fish and the group plotted the best way to catch a sea monster. And that was just the beginning!

With a little imagination, the possibilities are endless. This month's curriculum is filled with opportunities for children (and you!) to sail the high seas of imagination.

Imagination

Young children have incredibly rich imaginations, and love to pretend and play make-believe. They may be only just beginning to make distinctions between what is real and what is not, which makes early childhood one of the most magical times in life. The activities in this theme are designed to foster children's imaginations and expand their magical, creative fantasy worlds.

Imagination Station

Here are a few easy tips for fostering imagination in the classroom.

* Turn a large paper cone into a magical hat by gluing on bits of ribbon, yarn, cloth, beads, sequins, and glitter. Let children take turns wearing the hat at circle time as they make up stories.

* You can never have too many dress-up clothes, hats, puppets, and dolls available to nurture and encourage pretend play in the dramatic play area!

* What can you see in an inkblot? Splatter paint on paper, fold in half, unfold, and have children describe what they see.

Magical Hat Storytelling

Gather a variety of hats for children to wear, from baseball caps to firefighter's helmets. Tell children that today their hats will have magical, make-believe powers. When they put on their hats, children can become whatever they want!

Let children put on their hats, close their eyes, and listen to you as you begin a story: *Once upon a time there was a child who had a magical hat. Whenever he/she put on this hat, he/she turned into a...* Let children take turns filling in the blanks and adding to the story. Spark children's imaginations by asking questions such as *What special powers do you have when you put on your magical hat? Where can you go? Who do you meet?*

Create a class *Magic Hat* book by writing down children's tales and inviting them to add their own illustrations.

Imagination Bread

Imagine sitting high in a treehouse, sharing a piece of yummy chocolate-chip banana bread with a best friend. Or sailing the seas, enjoying a tropical fruit bread with coconut, bananas, and mango. Or living on Planet Orange, where people only eat their bread with mango, apricot, and peach chunks! Children can use their imaginations to transform this basic banana bread into whatever they want.

* 1 stick unsalted butter
* 1/3 cup brown sugar
* 1/3 cup white sugar
* 2 large eggs
* 1 teaspoon vanilla
* 2 large very ripe chopped bananas
* 1 cup white flour
* 3/4 cup whole wheat flour
* 2 teaspoons baking powder
* 1/2 teaspoon salt

"Imagination" Ingredients:

* chocolate chips
* walnuts
* raisins
* dried cranberries
* chopped prunes
* chopped apricots
* shredded coconut
* blueberries
* raspberries
* chopped strawberries
* mango
* pineapple or peaches (without juice)

1. Cream together butter and sugar.
2. Add eggs and vanilla; mix until just blended.
3. Add bananas and mix until fairly smooth.
4. Mix flour, baking powder, and salt together and add to the first mixture. Mix until just blended.
5. Add one cup of each of your chosen "imagination" ingredients. Mix briefly and pour batter in a 5- by 9-inch greased and floured loaf pan.
6. Bake at 350°F for one hour. Makes one large loaf or three small loaves.

Books can take you anywhere!

Cloudy with a Chance of Meatballs by Judi Barrett (Atheneum, 1978)

Harold's Circus by Crockett Johnson (HarperCollins, 1981)

Harold's Trip to the Sky by Crockett Johnson (HarperCollins, 1981)

The Maggie B by Irene Haas (McElderry, 1975)

Now What Can I Do? by Margaret Park Bridges (SeaStar, 2001)

Tuesday by David Wiesner (Clarion, 1991)

Where the Wild Things Are by Maurice Sendak (Harper & Row, 1976)

Harold's Purple Crayon

Read Crockett Johnson's classic *Harold and the Purple Crayon* (Harper & Row, 1955) and then let children create their own purple fantasy journey! You'll need a long sheet of white butcher paper and a purple crayon to create a mural of children's imaginings. To begin, ask, *Where will we go with our purple crayon today?* Invite children make up their own tale. You might use a box of magazine pictures (of interesting buildings, faraway places, animals, vehicles, and so on) to get started. Just pull out a picture at random and ask if children would like to incorporate it into their story.

Draw simple illustrations to represent children's ideas. When the story is complete, display the creation on a wall. Invite children to retell their adventure to family members at pick-up time.

Or, let children write their own version of Harold's Purple Crayon. Give each child a white sheet of paper and a selection of crayons. Write a title based on the child's name and chosen color (such as Holly's Orange Crayon) and draw a small stick figure at the upper left of the sheet. Then invite children to go on an adventure, just like Harold did!

Cloud Dreams

On a cloudy day, share *It Looked Like Spilt Milk* by Charles Shaw (HarperCollins, 1988) with children. Then go cloud-watching! Go outside and invite children to look at clouds as they make up their own versions of the story, for instance: *Sometimes it looked like a turtle, but it wasn't...*

As you look at the sky, talk with children about clouds. Ask: *What do you think clouds are made of? How do the clouds look today? Are they light and wispy, or thick and fluffy? Can you see any colors beside white in the clouds?* Later, have children make their own cloud pictures by sponge-painting on blue paper, using colors of their choice.

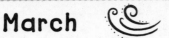

March Winds

In many climates, March is the time of year when the spring sun begins warming the earth and the air begins to move and circulate. In this theme, you will find plenty of outdoor activities to help children explore and learn about wind.

Parachute Storm!

To create a parachute storm, you will need a 12-foot parachute (or large sheet) and the help of another adult. Lay the parachute out flat on the ground, with the two adults standing on opposite sides. Have children stand evenly around the perimeter, holding the parachute with a "thumbs-up" grip (palms up, fingers underneath the edge of the parachute, and thumbs on top).

Begin by gently fluttering the parachute and softly saying: *I feel a gentle breeze. Do you feel it? Now I feel a stronger breeze. Do you feel it?* Repeat with the words *gust, gale, storm, hurricane, tornado,* and *monsoon,* shaking the parachute up and down with increasing speed. Add more detailed descriptions with each shake, such as: *I hear the clothes flapping on the line; the waves are huge; the trees are swaying;* and so on. Invite children to chime in with their own descriptions and sound effects as well.

When your parachute is flapping hard, say: *It's raining out! Everyone duck inside!* Lift the parachute high and let children sit underneath as you continue the story. End the story by shaking the parachute more and more gently as the winds calm down to a gentle breeze. Repeat, this time inviting children to help narrate the "wind story."

Straw Painting

Children can make their own wind art!

1. Mix 1 1/2 cups of water with several squirts of dishwashing liquid, and place a few tablespoons of the mixture on a sheet of white construction paper. Add a drop or two of food coloring, without mixing.

2. Provide children with straws and let them move and mix the water and food coloring by blowing it across the paper. Invite them to practice blowing strong gales and gentle breezes as they straw-paint.

Fly a Kite

Create a St. Patrick's Day kite!

1. Each child will need a paper grocery bag, two 18-inch lengths of string or ribbon for a handle, and strips of scrap paper or ribbon for a tail.

2. Have children decorate their bags with potato prints. Cut a potato in half (so that you get round "stamps") and let children dip the cut surface into green paint and press it onto the bag. Show children how to make a four-leaf clover by overlapping three or four circles.

3. When the bags are dry, fold the top of the bag one inch over for reinforcement and punch a hole in each of the four corners. Then crisscross and tie the two pieces of string to diagonal corners. Let children tape or glue the tails to the bottom of the bag.

4. On a windy day, take children outdoors and let them run with their kites behind them. Bring a camera and take photographs of your festive creations!

Wind Talk

Build background with children. Here are a few questions and discussion-starters:

✳ *Can you see the wind? Can you feel it? Can you touch it, hear it, smell it, or taste it?*

✳ *What happens when it is windy?*

✳ *Who needs wind?* (Sailors need wind to move their boats. Trees and flowers need wind too. The wind gives seeds and pollen a ride to a new place where they will sprout and grow.)

✳ *Can you make a breeze? Try folding a piece of paper like an accordion to make a fan.*

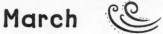

Move Like the Wind

The wind is a wonderful thing,
(hug body)

We never know what it will bring.
(shrug shoulders)

It can bring a seed so tiny and light,
(cup hands in front of body)

It can sway a big tree from left to right.
(sway arms overhead)

It can bring rain or hail or snow,
(move hands up and down in front of body)

It can move the clouds both fast and slow.
(twirl body around)

It can bring a ship from far at sea,
(hold hand at brow)

It can blow my kite away from me.
(wave hand overhead)

It can bring us warmth, it can bring us cold.
(fan face with hand and then rub hands)

It brings what it wants, and not what it's told.
(shake head up and down, side to side)

It can whisper or howl, it can even sing.
(make voice whisper and howl)

That's the wind, it's a wonderful thing.
(hug body)

—Annie Stiefel

Book Nook

Enjoy the cool breeze of a good book!

Catch the Wind: All About Kites by Gail Gibbons (Little Brown, 1995)

Gilberto and the Wind by Marie Hall Ets (Penguin Putnam, 1978)

How Does the Wind Walk? by Nancy Carlstrom (Simon & Schuster, 1993)

One Windy Wednesday by Phyllis Root (Candlewick. 1997)

What Can You Do in the Wind? by Anna Grossnickle Hines (Greenwillow, 1999)

The Wind Blew by Pat Hutchins (Simon & Schuster, l993)

The Wind's Garden by Bethany Roberts (Holt, 2003)

Wind Watchers

Help children observe the weather outdoors. Put a pinwheel just outside the window, hang a flag or chimes, or even hang a piece of crepe paper from a tree. Guide children to understand that the more these items move, the stronger the wind is.

The Shape of Things

Learning about shapes is an important first step on the road to developing reading and math skills. Being able to discern and name shapes gives children a firm foundation as they begin to decipher letters and numbers. These hands-on activities allow children to touch, manipulate, and experiment with real objects as they reinforce basic shape concepts.

Feely Box

A Feely Box is a wonderful sensory tool you can use all year long. It can help increase children's memory and communication skills, as well as fine-motor skills and tactile awareness.

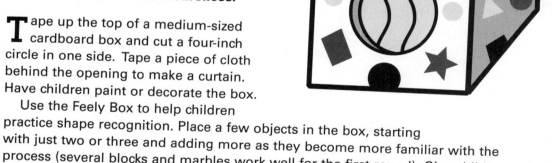

Tape up the top of a medium-sized cardboard box and cut a four-inch circle in one side. Tape a piece of cloth behind the opening to make a curtain. Have children paint or decorate the box.

Use the Feely Box to help children practice shape recognition. Place a few objects in the box, starting with just two or three and adding more as they become more familiar with the process (several blocks and marbles work well for the first round). Give children verbal directions, such as *Put your hand in the box. Find and pull out all the square objects in the box. Now see if you can find something round.* You might also try placing several plastic alphabet letters in the box and giving directions such as *Find the J for your name, Jessica.*

You can also use your Feely Box to tie in with your theme of the week. For example, if you're studying dinosaurs, place a few plastic dinosaurs in the box along with other objects, then challenge children to pick out the dinosaurs!

Recipe

Shape Cookies

Here is a basic sugar-cookie recipe, jazzed up with maple syrup.

Cookies make a wonderful, edible medium for introducing children to shapes: youngsters love patting and poking the dough and using shape cookie cutters. Sets of cutters can usually be found at kitchen shops or teacher supply stores, but you can also simply provide children with cardboard cut into simple shapes. Children can place the patterns on top of the dough and cut around them with plastic knives or craft sticks.

* 1 cup soft butter
* 1 cup light brown sugar
* 1 egg
* 1 tablespoon vanilla
* 3 tablespoons maple syrup
* 2 teaspoons baking soda
* 3 1/4 cups flour

Optional, for flavor: 2 tablespoons hot coffee (caffeine is neutralized during baking)

1. Cream together butter and sugar.

2. Add egg, vanilla, and syrup to the mixture.

3. Stir in baking soda (and coffee if desired).

4. Add flour to the mixture and blend.

5. Divide dough in half. Place each half in plastic wrap and pat into a 1/2-inch thick rectangle. Chill one hour.

6. Roll dough out to 1/4-inch thick and cut with cookie cutters. Bake at 350°F for eight minutes or until golden. Makes approximately two dozen large cookies.

Book Nook

Here are some great shape books to share with children:

Brown Rabbit's Shape Book by Alan Baker (Kingfisher, 1994)

Cubes, Cones, Cylinders, & Spheres by Tana Hoban (Greenwillow, 2000)

The Shape of Me and Other Stuff by Dr. Seuss (Random House, 1997)

The Shape of Things by Dayle Ann Dodds (Scott Foresman, 1996)

Shapes, Shapes, Shapes by Tana Hoban (Morrow, 1986)

So Many Circles, So Many Squares by Tana Hoban (Greenwillow, 1998)

A Star in My Orange: Looking for Nature's Shapes by Dana Meachen Rau (Millbrook, 2002)

Shape Up!

Build skills with these ideas.

* Talk about shapes in children's environment. *What shapes do you see around you? Who can find the triangle in the swing set?*

* Provide children with a variety of paper shapes in different sizes and colors. Invite children to put them together to create a person, a ship, a machine, or a space monster!

Shrink Art

To make shrink art, help children press cookie cutters (in various shapes) firmly onto clean, Styrofoam produce trays. Let children trace the outlines with permanent markers and then color the shapes. Cut out the shapes and punch a large hole at the top of each one, about the width of two pencils.

Place the shapes on a foil-lined cookie sheet and bake at 350°F for three minutes (make sure your cooking area is well-ventilated). Remove the cookie sheet from the oven and immediately uncurl the shapes (a toothpick works well) if necessary. You can hang the shrunken shapes with string from lights, windows, and trees, or use them to create a mobile.

Tiptoe to the Square

Collect square objects for children to explore, such as blocks, floor and wall tiles, carpet squares, and squares cut from cardboard, sandpaper, and other textured materials. Point out that each side of a square is the same length. Ask: *How many sides does a square have?* Help children trace the outlines of a few square objects onto paper and color them in.

To reinforce squares and other shapes, cut out five different large shapes from colored posterboard. Hang the shapes on the walls and furniture, or lay them on the floor. Choose one child to be the caller and call out directions, such as: *Tiptoe to the square. Jump to the triangle. Crawl to the oval. Walk to the circle.* Outdoors, running and galloping are also big favorites!

Rectangle Flags

Children can create colorful flags using wallpaper scraps, rectangular sponges, and paint. Ask a wallpaper store to save outdated sample books for you, and cut sponges into rectangles of different sizes. Explain that rectangles have four corners, two matching long sides and two matching short sides. Let each child choose a large, rectangular piece of wallpaper and decorate it with sponge paint prints. When dry, tape the flag to a cardboard paper towel or wrapping-paper tube. Then play some lively music and let children wave their flags in a rectangle parade!

Here Comes Spring

How do children know that spring is almost here? Has anyone seen a crocus, felt a warm breeze, or seen wild animals with their babies? Has the onion grass in the yard begun to sprout? Spring officially starts on or about March 20th, and children may have already begun to see the signs of the season. It's time to celebrate spring!

Use spring-related vocabulary at circle time. Introduce names of flowers and birds, and words like *thaw, soil,* and *seedling.*

Spring Weather

Weather changes noticeably in the spring, which makes it a good season to keep a weather calendar. Each afternoon, ask children what the day's weather was like: *Was it warm, hot, or cold? Sunny or cloudy? Windy or still? Did it rain or snow? Is the sky blue or gray?*

Record children's observations on a class calendar and compare them from day to day. If you kept a weather calendar the previous year, you might even compare this spring to last spring. Introduce new vocabulary words such as *humid* and *balmy* as the weather grows warmer. You might also introduce weather instruments such as a thermometer or weather vane. As children spot signs of spring, add them to your weather log as well.

Listening Walk

Read *The Listening Walk* by Paul Showers (HarperCollins, 1991), then take a listening walk of your own. You might pack a picnic snack and take a stroll around your yard or a neighborhood park. As you walk, encourage children to listen carefully. Make a list of each sound of spring you hear!

Everything's Sprouting!

Children love watching things come to life, and lentils are fun and easy to sprout.

1. Measure 1/3 cup of lentils and soak overnight in a bowl or container of four cups warm water. Drain, rinse with fresh water, and place lentils in a quart jar.

2. Cover with a dampened piece of cheesecloth (held in place with a rubber band), and store in a dark cupboard. Rinse twice a day (add cool water and then drain thoroughly, making sure all excess water is drained each time).

3. By the third day, the lentils will sprout. Sample them at snack time—they're a great source of protein and vitamins!

March Lion-Lambs

This project illustrates the old folk saying "March comes in like a lion and goes out like a lamb."

1. Each child will need two white paper plates. Use wiggly eyes, paper scraps, glue, crayons, and markers on each plate to make a lion face and a lamb face.

2. For the lion, children can use yellow yarn or strips of yellow paper for a mane (they apply glue around the edge of the plate and attach the yarn or paper). Help them glue short pieces of pipe cleaner or uncooked spaghetti for whiskers. Let dry.

3. For the lamb, have children glue cotton balls around the face, creating a woolly coat. Let dry.

4. Glue or staple the plates together, so that both animal faces show. Attach a string at the top for hanging on a doorknob at home. Make an extra face to hang in the classroom. Each day, let a different child choose the animal face that best illustrates the weather and turn it face out. You might keep a chart of how many "lion days" and how many "lamb days" occur in the month of March. This project provides a great opportunity to introduce opposites: *a loud lion, a quiet lamb; a gentle breeze, a powerful wind; cold weather, warm weather*; and so on.

Will It Sprout?

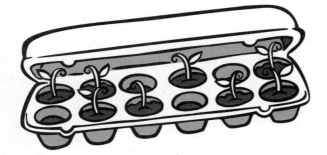

1. Where can seeds sprout? To find out, take an empty styrofoam egg carton and fill each hole with something different: a damp paper towel, soil, and ten other substances of children's choosing (sand, ketchup, coffee, water, peanut butter, and so on—children love choosing the substances!)

2. Place seeds in each hole (grass seed, bean seeds, and radish seeds work well).

3. Have children make predictions and observe each day. You'll find that seeds can grow anywhere damp!

Book Nook

What else might spring bring? Find out with a good book!

Come to the Meadow by Anna Grossnickle Hines (Houghton Mifflin, 1984)

It's Spring by Linda Glaser (Millbrook, 2002)

My Spring Robin by Anne Rockwell (Aladdin, 1996)

Paperwhite by Nancy Elizabeth Wallace (Houghton Mifflin, 2000)

Spring Song by Barbara Seuling (Gulliver, 2001)

When Spring Comes by Natalie Kinsey-Warnock (Dutton, 1993)

When Will It Be Spring? by Catherine Walters (Dutton, 2001)

Seeing Spring

Celebrate spring colors with these quick and easy ideas.

* Take easels outside, along with some blue, yellow, and white paint. See how many different shades of green children can spot in your yard, and then let them create their own shades of green by mixing the paints on the paper!

* Cut shapes from pastel tissue paper. Have children paint a thin layer of water-glue mixture on a sheet of waxed paper, then lay down bits of tissue. Hang in a window for "spring stained glass"! (For an added spring touch, add floral-scented perfume to the water-glue mixture.)

Buds Are Beautiful

Bring in a few budding branches and watch them bloom! Forsythia, pussy willow, apple, or maple buds will work well. Place branches in a container of water in a sunny window and let children examine the buds with a magnifying glass each day. Every few days, change the water and cut a half-inch off the bottom of the stems. The branches will bloom within one to two weeks!

Dessert for the Birds

Celebrate spring by making a cake for your feathered friends.

Line clean tuna cans (no lids) or similarly-shaped plastic containers with plastic wrap. Let children fill the liners with vegetable shortening, and chill for half an hour. Then remove the "bird cake" by lifting the plastic wrap from the can. Let children decorate their cakes with seeds, nuts, cornmeal, bread, and bits of fruit and vegetable peelings. They can add a pretzel-stick "candle" for a finishing touch. Remove plastic, set the cakes outside in a spot that's visible from your window, and watch as the birds arrive at the party!

Green Veggies

Spring has arrived and everything is coming up green!

Set out a spread of fresh green vegetables and let children taste each. Together, make a graph of children's favorites. Choose a few of the following:

* Broccoli
* Green beans
* Snap peas
* Scallions
* Celery
* Asparagus
* Green pepper
* Zucchini
* Bok choi
* Lettuce (various kinds)
* Spinach

Point out that green comes in different shades, and each vegetable is slightly different in color. Explain that green vegetables are an important part of a healthy diet!

For Reading Out Loud!

The first time a child reads a book by him or herself is a momentous occasion. My heart still skips a beat whenever I remember a return trip from the library with my then five-year-old son, Zach. His excited shout from the back seat, "Mom…I'm reading! I'm reading! All by myself!" caused me to pull over and stop the car. I was just as excited as he was.

For most adults, reading is so familiar that we often forget the wonder and the thrill of learning to decipher the written word. But to a child, learning to read is as exciting as taking first steps or riding a bicycle without training wheels.

Since National Library Week occurs in April, it's the perfect time to focus on reading and helping children develop a love of written language. Once you've established the read-aloud habit, you'll see children's listening and language skills increase!

For Reading Out Loud

There is one very simple thing you can do to help children build the language and listening skills necessary for reading: Read aloud to them every day. Read with feeling. Give each character a different voice. Vary the selections and return to old favorites as well. If you read to children regularly and give them the opportunity to interact with an enthusiastic reader (you!), chances are they'll learn to love reading themselves.

A Book-Friendly Environment

Creating a book-friendly environment in your home or classroom not only imparts the message that books are important, it also gives young children the message that they are important. Part of the enjoyment of a child's early reading experience is the time spent snuggling on an adult's lap, or sitting with a cozy group at story time.

Display books at children's eye level so children can handle and play with books. As they look at, touch, and turn each page, they begin to absorb what reading and writing are all about.

Story Time Magic

Make story time a relaxed and enjoyable experience, and let children be drawn to the sound of your voice. If story time seems to be dragging, spice it up! You might have a special package marked "Story Time Magic" at the reading nook. Inside, pack a special blanket or colorful sheet, a story time mascot or prop (a stuffed animal, a puppet, or a simple musical instrument), and some irresistible new books. The blanket can serve as a magic carpet for the group to sit on whenever they take a journey through a book, the mascot can help signal that story time is about to begin, and each new book will open the magic doorway to a reading adventure.

In general, fifteen minutes is a good length of time to read to a young group. Encourage children's participation by asking questions such as: *What do you think will happen next?* or *What was your favorite part?* You can also let children take turns choosing a book for story time each day.

So, let the magical journey begin. Open a book and step right in!

Books, Books, Books

A book is a vehicle that can take you outside your classroom, town, or even your country! Invite children to go "book traveling" this week. Let them choose books from your shelves for reading aloud. Then hop aboard and let each book transport children to a new world. If it's a story they know well, you might suggest that they close their eyes as you read. What pictures did children see while their eyes were closed?

Book Share

Invite children to share their favorite books.

Have family members help children choose a favorite book to bring in. Also have a stack of books available for children who were not able to bring one to school. When you have gathered the selections, show children how to make bookmarks. Have them decorate 2- by 6-inch strips of oaktag or lightweight cardboard with rubber stamps and ink pads, stickers, or markers (one side only). Punch a hole at the top and add a yarn tassel.

Throughout the day, read the books children brought to share. Ask children what they like best about the book they brought, and write the title of the book and their comments on the back of their bookmarks. Label the bookmarks with children's names and the date, and send them home tucked inside the books!

A Trip to the Library

Plan a visit to your local library. In preparation for your trip, talk with children about what they can expect to see there. Ask: *What are libraries for? Why do we speak quietly in the library? What kinds of books will we be able to borrow?* Children may even be able to get their own library cards.

Before you visit, ask the librarian to talk with children about his or her job, show them where to find their favorite books, and read a story to the group. Follow up your visit with a class-made thank-you card, complete with a photograph of the group on their trip and a drawing or message from the children.

Great literature never goes out of style! Here are some classics perfect for reading aloud.

Caps for Sale by Esphyr Slobodkina (HarperCollins, 1947)

Corduroy by Don Freeman (Viking, 1968)

Goodnight Moon by Margaret Wise Brown (HarperCollins, 1976)

A House Is a House for Me by Mary Ann Hoberman (Viking, 1978)

Millions of Cats by Wanda Gag (Putnam, 1997)

The Runaway Bunny by Margaret Wise Brown (HarperCollins, 1972)

The Story about Ping by Marjorie Flack (Viking, 1961)

The Very Hungry Caterpillar by Eric Carle (Philomel, 1969)

Where the Wild Things Are by Maurice Sendak (HarperCollins, 1976)

Bookends

Children can create bookends to keep their favorite books standing straight and tall!

1. For each bookend, you will need two 2 1/2 cups (one pound) of plaster of paris, one cup of water, and a pint-sized milk carton.

2. Mix the plaster and water and quickly pour it into the carton. Let harden for several hours and then peel off the carton. Children can paint their bookends and add glitter, stickers, and other decorations.

3. When children are finished decorating their bookends, label the bottom of each with the child's name and the date.

Story Basket

Here is a fun storytelling tradition to start with children. Collect plastic figures, stuffed animals, dolls, puppets, and other small props and place them in a basket. As you read any given story, invite children to act it out using props from the basket.

Classroom Reading Tips

✳ Vary your book selections. Choose from fiction and nonfiction, poetry and prose. Look for books illustrated with a variety of paintings, drawings, and photographs.

✳ Talk with children about ways in which all books are the same (covers, pages, words) and ways in which they are different.

✳ Encourage children to chime in when they know the words to a favorite story, or on repeated refrains. This is a great way to make children part of the reading experience.

✳ Reading aloud can also help at transition times. Share a story or a few poems to help children wind down and get them ready for the next activity.

Clip-a-Story

Let children cut out pictures from magazines and catalogs (the pictures might feature children, adults, animals, plants, places, foods, vehicles, toys, and so on). Children can glue the pictures to sheets of construction paper to create book pages. Then let each child choose one page as the starting point for a story. Invite them to narrate the story while you write it down on each page (they can add more pictures and hand-drawn details). Spark ideas with questions such as: *Where is the puppy going? Why is the boy smiling?*
When finished, have children think of a title, create a cover, and then bind their pages together into little books.

Need help selecting a book? Here are some excellent sources to guide you:

The New York Times Parent's Guide to the Best Books for Children by Eden Ross Lipson (Times Books, 2000)

The Read-Aloud Handbook, 5th Edition by Jim Trelease (Penguin, 2001)

Read to Me: Raising Kids Who Love to Read by Bernice E. Cullinan (Scholastic, 2000)

To receive a free, unique, and well-organized children's book catalog, call Chinaberry Books at 800-776-2242.

Bunny Fun

Young children are fascinated by animals and love to watch, pet, cuddle, and feed them! Rabbits are soft and gentle—and particularly appealing to young children. If possible, bring children to a farm or petting zoo to see a real rabbit. Or, if anyone in your group has a pet bunny that likes interacting with people, you might ask the family to bring it in for a visit.

Peek-a-Boo Bunny

1. Each child will need two white paper plates. Let children paint one side of both (you might use white, brown, and black and have children mix them into different shades) and have them glue pre-cut black or pink paper eyes and a nose to one.

2. Have children add pipe cleaners or toothpicks for whiskers. Cut the edges off the second paper plate to create the bunny's ears. Overlap the ears as shown, and place them on the bunny's face. Then push a brass brad through all three layers.

3. Invite children to move the ears downward, then up again to reveal the bunny's face.

Bunny Match-Up

Children can create bunny pairs and then match them by texture.

1. Each child will need two bunny shapes (see above right for example) cut from lightweight cardboard or oaktag. Have children color their pairs. Provide children with an assortment of "bunny tails," such as cotton balls, pom poms, buttons, colored dot stickers, milk caps, sandpaper circles, and velvet circles.

2. Let each child choose a type of tail and glue one to each of their bunnies so they have a matching pair. Write the child's name on the back of each bunny.

3. When the bunnies are finished, sit with children in a circle and have them each put one of their bunnies in the middle. Then take one bunny and pass it around the circle for children to feel. Have children close their eyes and feel the bunnies (then open their eyes) to find their matching pairs. Repeat with the remaining bunnies until each child is reunited with his or her bunny (they will need to open their eyes and check their names, since some children may have chosen the same type of tail).

Did You Ever See a Bunny?

Build gross motor skills as you do a bunny hop!

Cut two bunny ears from stiff paper for each child. Let children decorate the ears with tempera paints, puff paints, or cotton balls. When dry, staple the ears to a paper strip and fit the strip around children's heads to make a bunny-ear headband. Let children wear their bunny ears as they hop around and act out this bunny song.

(To the tune of "Did You Ever See a Lassie?")

Did you ever see a bunny, a bunny, a bunny,

Did you ever see a bunny that hops up and down?

It hops and it hops and it hops and it hops,

Did you ever see a bunny that hops up and down?

When children are familiar with the song, invite them to come up with new movements and verses by substituting the phrase *hops up and down* with different actions, such as *scurries through the fields*, *nibbles the grass*, *gnaws on a carrot*, and so on.

Row of Rabbits

Children will build their understanding of addition and subtraction concepts as you act out this poem on a feltboard. Cut out five rabbit shapes from felt. Then recite the poem, adding and removing the appropriate number of rabbits as you go. As children become familiar with the poem, invite them to take turns coming up to the board and adding and removing the rabbits themselves. To turn the poem into a movement activity, let children put on their rabbit ears (see page 119) and act out the poem.

A row of little rabbits standing here by me,
How many rabbits do you see?
Two jumped up and away they go.
Now how many rabbits in the row?
One hops away when it begins to snow.
How many rabbits in the row?
This one leaves when the wind begins to blow.
Now how many rabbits in the row?
One comes back, now do you know
How many rabbits in the row?
One comes back to see the show,
How many rabbits in the row?
Two come back to the line and so...
How many rabbits in the row?

Book Nook

Share classic and new bunny books.

The Country Bunny and the Little Gold Shoes by Dubose Heyward (Houghton Mifflin, 1939)

Ella and the Rabbit by Helen Cooper (Crocodile Books, 1990)

I Am a Bunny by Ole Rissom (Golden, 1967)

Seven Little Rabbits by John Becker (Walker, 1973)

So Many Bunnies: A Bedtime ABC and Counting Book by Rick Walton (Lothrop, 1998)

The Tale of Peter Rabbit by Beatrix Potter (Warne, 1902)

Too Many Hopkins by Tomie dePaola (Putnam, 1989)

Bunny Banter

As children explore bunnies, invite them to think about the questions below.

✳ What do you think rabbits eat?

✳ Where do you think they live?

✳ What colors do rabbits come in?

✳ Do you think rabbits make any sounds?

✳ What does a baby bunny look like? How does it change as it grows?

✳ Would you like a rabbit for a pet? Why or why not?

Recipe

Carrot Soup

Colorful, crunchy, and naturally sweet, carrots are good for bunnies and children alike!

* ✳ 2 tablespoons butter or olive oil
* ✳ 1 pound carrots, peeled and sliced
* ✳ 1 large onion, chopped
* ✳ 1 clove garlic, minced
* ✳ 1/2 cup raw rice
* ✳ 1 teaspoon sugar
* ✳ 6 cups chicken or vegetable stock
* ✳ juice of 1 orange
* ✳ 3/4 cup milk or cream

1. Heat the butter or oil in a saucepan and saute the carrots, onion, and garlic for 10 minutes.

2. Add the rice, sugar, and chicken stock to the pan and bring to a boil (supervise closely for safety). Then cover and simmer for 20 minutes.

3. Let cool, then show children how to use a potato masher to "puree" the soup in the pot. Add juice and milk or cream.

4. Return to heat and season to taste with salt and pepper. Makes three quarts.

Here Is a Bunny

This fingerplay helps develop small motor control, eye-hand coordination, and language skills.

Here is a bunny,
(*hold up index and middle finger*)

With ears so funny,
(*bend index and middle fingers*)

And here is a hole in the ground.
(*make a circle with thumb and index and middle fingers of other hand*)

When a noise he hears
(*ask a child to clap or bang a drum once*)

He pricks up his ears,
(*straighten up bunny-ear fingers*)

And into his hole disappears.
(*poke bunny-ear fingers into hole*)

For extra fun, draw three dots for eyes and a nose (with non-toxic marker) on children's upper palms just below the bunny-ear fingers, and attach cotton balls with double-sided tape to the backs of their hands for bunny tails. Then have them join you in the chant!

Backyard Birds

Children enjoy feeding and watching birds all year long, but spring is a special time for observing them. In many regions at this time of year, migrating birds such as robins and hummingbirds begin to return north. Encourage children to stay on the lookout for the first birds to make their way back to your skies.

Fun Feathered Facts

Share these fun facts with children:

* ✳ Birds called grebes build floating nests on water. Many birds build nests in trees, but birds also build nests in the ground, on eaves, and in cattails!

* ✳ Some birds do not build their own nests—they put their eggs in the nests of other birds.

* ✳ The largest bird in the world is the ostrich (up to 300 pounds), native to Africa. They also lay the largest eggs, up to eight inches long!

* ✳ The smallest bird in the world is the Cuban bee hummingbird (2 1⁄4 inches in length from bill to tail).

* ✳ The largest bird in North America is the trumpeter swan (about 28 pounds).

* ✳ The whooping crane is the tallest bird, standing almost five feet.

* ✳ The peregrine falcon is the fastest bird, flying at speeds up to 220 miles per hour!

* ✳ There are more than 9,000 different species of birds.

Fly Like a Bird

Do you wish you could fly? Enrich the dramatic play center with bird-related props: towels for kids to drape over shoulders and flap like wings, materials for nest-building (yarn, shredded paper, string, tinsel), some branches, a bird whistle, an empty box of birdseed, a small bird house...even rubber worms!

Spring Fling

Read Anne Rockwell's *Our Yard Is Full of Birds* (Simon & Schuster, 1992) and then throw a party for your feathered friends!

✳ Let children toss seeds and crumbs on the ground, along with scraps of yarn or dryer lint for nest-building materials.

✳ Create a birdbath by lining the bottom of a large shallow container with pebbles, filling it with water, and laying it on the ground.

✳ Show children how to call the birds by making a loud kissing sound with their lips on the back of their hands. If possible, share a pair of binoculars. Also bring along a bird-identification book or field guide, and help children identify their "guests."

Bird Watch

✳ Watch for birds building nests, plucking worms, or pecking seeds from the ground. Listen for their distinct calls. How many birds can children identify?

✳ Contact the Audubon Society (www.audubon.org) for inexpensive bird-callers, identification guides, and feeding charts.

✳ Children may have family members who bird-watch as a hobby. Many bird-watchers keep "life books" of their sightings and can share their records with the group.

Zip a Feather

What makes birds different from all other animals? Birds are the only animals with feathers! Bring in some bird feathers. You can find one on the ground outside (wash it off once inside), or simply purchase real feathers at a craft store.

Let children examine the feathers. As they explore, ask questions such as: *What do the feathers feel like? What sorts of patterns do you see? Are the feathers different sizes and shapes?* Let children try dipping a feather in water. What happens? Explain that birds' feathers work like a raincoat to help keep them dry. Then show children how to run their thumbs and index fingers up and down the side of a feather, "zipping and unzipping" the individual strands.

You might also explain that feathers were used as pens long ago. Let children try to write with the tip of a feather dipped in paint, or use the side of the feather as a paintbrush. Leave the feathers in the dramatic play center for children to use as props.

Book Nook

Fly away with books!

About Birds: A Guide for Children by John Sill (Peachtree, 1991)

Are You My Mother? by P.D. Eastman (Random House, 1960)

The Bird Nest by P.D. Eastman (Random House, 1968)

Cradle in the Trees by Pat Demoth (Simon & Schuster, 1994)

Feathers for Lunch by Lois Ehlert (Harcourt, 1993)

Make Way for Ducklings by Robert McCloskey (Viking, 1941)

25 Birds Every Child Should Know by Jim Arnosky (Bradbury, 1993)

Chicks & Bugs

Children never seem to tire of this delightful play-along poem. It gives them a chance to act out a simple subtraction concept and a good workout as well!

Let five children play the chicks and five play the bugs as they act out this poem in a large, outdoor play area. If there are fewer than 10 children in your group, simply cut out large paper bugs and scatter them around the yard for children to "chase." You might also create felt chicks and bugs, and use them to act out the poem on a feltboard.

Five little chicks by the old barn door,
one chased a beetle and then there were four.
Four little chicks under a tree,
one chased an ant and then there were three.
Three little chicks looking for something new,
one spied a grasshopper, then there were two.
Two little chicks said, "Oh, what fun!"
One ran after a ladybug, then there was one.
One little chick began to run
after a worm and then there were none.

Incredible Eggs

Children are most familiar with chickens' eggs, but remind them that birds' eggs come in all sizes, from tiny wrens' eggs to enormous ostrich eggs—and in all colors!

If you keep your eyes on the treetops this month, you might be able to spot a bird atop its nest. Watch the nest (from a distance) and observe signs of new life. Frequent trips by the mother bird for food—and lots of little peeps—mean babies have hatched. If you live in a city, check for birds' nests in protected spots, under building eaves, in the rafters of a subway station, or tucked in a crevice of a statue!

Eggs of Every Color

Egg decorating is an ancient tradition in many cultures. Here's one way to turn eggs into beautifully colored works of art.

Have each child place a hardboiled egg (with or without its shell; either will work) in the center of an 8-inch square piece of damp cheesecloth. Help the child gather the cloth tightly around the egg and secure it with a twist-tie.

Mix several bowls of food coloring with two or three tablespoons of vinegar and let children use eye droppers to squeeze drops of different colors onto the cloth. Wait a few hours for the eggs to dry. Then unwrap the cloth to reveal a bright multi-colored egg. Place the eggs in birds' nests (see page 126).

Birds' Nests

These birds' nests make a nice home for children's dyed eggs.

Make your favorite playdough (one that will air dry) or mix up a batch of Treedust Playdough (see page 127). Supply some soft, colorful mix-ins to add to the dough—yarn or ribbon scraps, dryer lint, string, straw, bits of tissue paper, and so on. Help young children form a nest by patting pieces of the dough onto the bottom of a small overturned bowl. Then help them remove the nest and line it with more of the "mix-ins." To dry, place the nests in a sunny spot for several days or bake at 200°F for one to two hours.

If you have any leftover mix-ins, let children stuff them into mesh onion bags to hang outside. Neighborhood birds will use them to line their nests!

Crack Open a Good Book!

Chickens Aren't the Only Ones by Ruth Heller (Grosset, 1981) is intensely colorful and has a fun, bouncy rhythm. Read it and you'll find out that chickens aren't the only ones to hatch from eggs!

Eggheads!

Carefully break the top off an egg. Empty it, rinse, fill with potting soil, and sprinkle on some grass seed. Add eyes, nose, and mouth with marker. Place in an empty egg carton. Water it, and within several days your little egg will sprout a head of "hair"!

Recipe

Treedust Play Dough

Ask families or a local lumberyard to save you a bag of "treedust" (fine sawdust) to recycle into play dough. (Make sure it does not come from pressure-treated lumber, which is toxic.)

* ❊ 2 cups fine sawdust
* ❊ 1 cup flour
* ❊ water (approximately 1 cup)

1. Mix sawdust and flour together in a bowl. Add water slowly until dough becomes a workable consistency.
2. Form dough into shapes or pat out and cut with cookie cutters.
3. Let it air dry in the sun for two to three days or bake at 200°F for one to two hours. Sand the shapes smooth and paint if desired.

Book Nook

Settle into the nest with a good story.

Daisy and the Egg by Jane Simmons (Little, Brown, 1999)

Egg Story by Anca Hariton (Dutton, 1992)

The Golden Egg Book by Margaret Wise Brown (Golden, 2000)

Good Morning, Chick by Mirra Ginsberg (Greenwillow, 1980)

Here a Chick, There a Chick by Bruce McMillan (Lothrop, 1983)

Horton Hatches the Egg by Dr. Seuss (Random House, 1966)

Alphabet Eggs

Have an indoor egg hunt!

Cut out enough pastel construction paper eggs so that each child will have one egg for every letter in his or her name. Write the letters of each child's name, putting one letter on each egg. Have children color the eggs with crayons or markers. Hide the eggs while children are out of the room.

Put on some lively music and let the hunt begin! When children have found all the eggs, put them together in one large pile and help children find the eggs with the letters of their name. Children can then glue the lettered eggs, in order, onto a sheet of paper. You can also mount eggs on your bulletin board or classroom door.

Egg-cellent Bread Pudding

This wonderfully creamy custard melts in your mouth and gives everyone plenty of egg-cracking practice!

* 12 slices of French bread, 1-inch thick
* butter
* 5 whole eggs
* 4 egg yolks
* 1 cup sugar
* 1/8 teaspoon salt
* 4 cups milk
* 1 cup heavy cream
* 2 teaspoons vanilla

1. Butter bread on one side. Place in a two-quart baking dish, buttered side up, overlapping the slices.

2. Mix together all the eggs, sugar, and salt, and set aside.

3. Heat milk and cream in a saucepan until just scalding (supervise children closely).

4. Pour gradually into the egg mixture, stirring well. Add vanilla.

5. Pour the milk/egg mixture over the bread. Place the baking dish inside a larger roasting pan. Add about one inch of water to the roasting pan.

6. Bake at 375°F about 45 minutes, until a fork inserted comes out clean. Makes 15 servings, 1/3 cup each.

Tap, Tap, Tap

Teach children how to tap an egg against the edge of a bowl until they hear and feel a crack, and then how to gently open it using two hands. Make sure children wash their hands thoroughly before and after. Use all your eggs to make a tasty omelet or Egg-cellent Bread Pudding (left).

Eggshell Art

Use eggshells to decorate paper shapes and holiday cutouts. Start by washing the eggshells thoroughly and laying them out on paper towels to dry. Then place the eggshells in a plastic self-sealing bag and let children gently crush them; the shell pieces should be small, but not too fine. Divide the

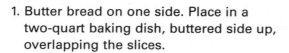

shells among four cups, cover them with rubbing alcohol, and add a few drops of different food colorings. Let them sit overnight. Then pour off the liquid and spread the shells out on a paper bag. Place them in the sun or a warm oven to dry.

Give children egg shapes in different sizes cut from stiff paper. Very young tots love to drizzle glue in random patterns and sprinkle on the colored shells. Older children enjoy making more elaborate designs.

The Magic of Gardening

My group was playing outdoors when I heard three-year-old Zoë calling "Annie, Annie...quick! Come see!" She was in the garden, jumping up and down with excitement. I ran to see what she had discovered. "The strawberry plant has a baby!" she exclaimed as she showed me a tiny green strawberry. By then all the children had gathered to look, and were calling out questions and comments: "Can we eat it? It's so little. Is it plastic? It's green! It's supposed to be red. Will the sun turn it red? Maybe it needs a drink."

It was our second year of gardening as a group, but our first year planting strawberries. We had carefully planted 10 strawberry plants the month before. The children had been intrigued by the runners that grew from the plants; they called them octopus legs. They had noticed the flowers, too. We had talked about the life cycle, from seed to plant to flower, and finally to fruit and seed again. We had also read about this cycle in several of our gardening stories, but now children were seeing it firsthand.

To children, it's pure magic to see a strawberry grow from a plant, or to have a dry bulb they buried in the fall emerge as a brilliant flower months later. Underground plants are magical too: a tiny peanut seed can turn into 30 or 40 more peanuts, complete with shells, all beneath the earth!

Digging in the Dirt

Most children love to work with soil. It is dark, rich, soft, and has a distinct, fresh smell. If you have not yet given children the opportunity to dig in the dirt, this spring might be the perfect time to start a garden with your group.

Science . . . on Your Hands and Knees

As children plant and nurture a garden, they learn that plants need good, rock-free soil, sunlight, and the right amount of water to survive and thrive. In a chemical-free garden, children can also see the food chain up close and in action. They will learn which creatures are the garden's friends and which ones are its foes. For instance, they might see aphids eating their tomatoes, but they might also see praying mantises coming to the rescue! The mantises will eat the aphids and save the tomato plants.

By working in the garden, children will not only learn about the cycles of life, but they'll also begin to develop an appreciation for the natural environment. As an extra benefit, you may also notice that young children are more willing to try a new vegetable when they've grown it themselves!

As your garden grows, you can keep children's interest blooming by varying your activities as well as your crops. Why not bring out your favorite puppet to help with the weeding? Try having a snack or lunch in your garden one day, or lay out some carpet squares and have story time amidst the flowers. Try a new crop each year, from a green bean tepee to a pumpkin patch. And don't forget to make room for a stool or bench. It's the perfect spot for watching your garden grow!

A Child's Garden

Gardening is a wonderful way to observe the cycle of life. As children prepare the soil, plant seeds and seedlings, water them, and watch and wait to see what happens, they'll learn what plants need to survive—then reap the rewards of beautiful flowers or delicious fruits and vegetables. When you garden with children, you give them the chance to experience the satisfaction of working the warm earth, harvesting what they sow, and the simple pleasures of nature. No room for a garden? Many flowers, herbs, and vegetables can be grown successfully in large pots or tubs.

Prepare Your Garden

Start by finding a sunny, well-drained area and then prepare your soil. After you have loosened the earth, give children buckets and shovels and let them dig for rocks and remove them. Children will enjoy turning peat moss or compost into the soil, too. Next, mark off your rows in the soil for planting. You can create paths by placing flat rocks, boards, or hay between the rows. This will help protect growing plants from little feet.

Begin a garden diary with children, recording what you plant and when and where you plant it. Also make a record of when the seeds germinate and tiny plants pop up through the soil. Measure your plants on a regular basis and track the measurements in your log as well. You can also write down all the insects and animals children observe in their garden. Throughout the growing season, take photographs of children tending to the garden and enjoying the fruits of their labors. Place the photos in the diary and you'll have a wonderful "How Our Garden Grows" book to share with families.

Sow Some Herbs

Give children's sense of smell a good workout by planting some herbs in your garden. Chives, basil, dill, rosemary, and lemon mint are a few easy herbs to try. (You will only need to plant lemon mint once, as it comes up each year thereafter on its own.) When the herbs have sprouted, show children how to gently rub the leaves and then sniff their fingers.

Try using your herbs at snack time. Lemonade is even more refreshing with a sprig of mint. You can also use your herbs to liven up tuna and pasta salads.

Gardening Aprons

These colorful aprons, printed with fruits and vegetables, makes gardening a special occasion while protecting clothes.

Each child will need a white cotton carpenter's apron (these are inexpensive and available at home supply stores). Gather an assortment of fabric paints, and spread the paints in shallow dishes or foam trays.

Provide children with a variety of fruits and vegetables for printing. Cut carrots into disks. Cut peppers, apples, lemons, and small oranges in half (cut citrus fruits the day before to allow them to dry slightly.) Mushrooms and broccoli florets work too. Insert a fork into each fruit and vegetable to use as a handle. Then let children dip the fruits and vegetables into the fabric paint, blot once on a damp sponge, and press onto the apron. Be sure to let the paint dry thoroughly before children wear their aprons.

Plant Your Favorites

Collect seed packets or seedlings and let children choose the ones they want to plant. Guide them as to how deep and how far apart to plant the seeds and seedlings in the soil. (For example: Poke a hole in the soil half a finger deep. Space the seeds four fingers apart.) Let children take turns watering the garden, showing them how they can tell when the plants have had enough. If the soil is light, it needs more water. If it's moist and dark like chocolate cake, it's just right!

Gather the packets from the seeds you used, or make simple line drawings on index cards of the fruits, vegetables, and flowers you planted. Laminate the cards or seed packets and attach them to craft sticks. Place your signs in the garden to mark the location of your plants.

Make a Scarecrow

A child-size scarecrow is lots of fun to make. Work together to make one for your school garden.

In advance, gather some old children's clothes. Stuff the clothes with hay (available at garden centers) or newspaper. You can attach shirts to pants with a few staples. Mount your scarecrow on a stick, an old broom, or a yardstick, using a stuffed nylon stocking for the head. Top off your scarecrow with a straw hat! You can also tie tin cans or pie plates to strong string and hang them on the scarecrow to keep the crows away.

Book Nook

Here are a few great books to grow on.

Alison's Zinnia by Anita Lobel (Greenwillow, 1990)

The Carrot Seed by Ruth Krauss (Harper & Row, 1945)

Growing Vegetable Soup by Lois Ehlert (Harcourt, 1987)

One Bean by Anne Rockwell (Walker, 1998)

Planting a Rainbow by Lois Ehlert (Harcourt, 1988)

Roots, Shoots, Buckets & Boots: Gardening Together with Children by Sharon Lovejoy (Workman, 1999)

The Rose in My Garden by Arnold Lobel (William Morrow, 1984)

Gardening Tips

✳ Attract butterflies to your garden with nectar-rich flowers, such as asters, hollyhocks, forget-me-nots, candytuft, and butterfly weed.

✳ If this is your first gardening experience, start small and keep it simple. These are all easy to grow: carrots, cucumbers, zucchini, beans, peppers, strawberries, watermelon, cherry tomatoes, and snow peas.

✳ You can brighten and define your garden with borders of marigolds, cosmos, zinnias, snap dragons, and petunias.

Mothers

Every mother is special to her baby, whether that baby is a kitten, a puppy, a llama, or a child! In this theme, you'll find activities that celebrate the unique relationship between mothers and children, as well as providing a lovely lead-in to Mother's Day. As you organize Mother's Day activities, keep in mind children's diverse family situations and bring sensitivity to your planning.

Where's My Baby?

Children love making animal noises and imitating the behaviors of their favorite creatures. With this hide-and-seek game, they get to do just that!

1. Ask one child to decide what kind of animal mother (or father) he or she would like to be. Then invite the rest of the group to play the animal babies. For instance, if the first child chooses a dog, the other children become the puppies. Have the mother cover her eyes while the puppies hide around the room or play yard.

2. Once the puppies have hidden, let the mother come out to search for the babies. Encourage the child to make the animal's sound (in this case, barking) and listen for the sound of her puppies barking back.

3. When the mother dog has found all her babies, it's the next mother's turn. Fun mother-baby pairs are owl/owlet, seal/pup, or goose/gosling. You might also add stuffed animal babies and dolls, plus books with pictures of all kinds of babies, to the dramatic play center.

Mother May I?

Here's a fun animal version of this old favorite.

1. In advance, draw simple pictures of a dog, a worm, a frog, a horse, a turtle, and a dinosaur, each on a separate piece of cardboard. Explain to children that the dog represents a four-legged walk, the worm a belly crawl, the frog a jumping step, the horse a run, the turtle a small-stepped walk, and the dinosaur a large-stepped walk. You can add on your own animal cards and steps as well.

2. Start off the game by playing the part of the mother yourself. Stand about 20 feet from children and hold up a card. Choose a volunteer and say, for example: *Nick, you may take giant dinosaur steps to me.* The child then asks: *Mother, may I?* When you answer *Yes, you may,* the child then takes giant dinosaur steps until he reaches you. Then it is that child's turn to hold up a new card and give another child directions.

3. When children are familiar with the game, vary it by answering *No* and then changing cards, for example: *No, you may not, but you may (hold up another card) wiggle like a worm!*

Book Nook

Here are some favorite "Mommy" books to share.

Are You My Mother? by P.D. Eastman (Random House, 1960)

Blueberries for Sal by Robert McCloskey (Viking, 1948)

A Chair for My Mother by Vera B. Williams (Greenwillow, 1982)

Is Your Mama a Llama? by Deborah Guarino (Scholastic, 1989)

Mama, Do You Love Me? by Barbara Joosse (Chronicle, 2001)

A Mother for Choco by Keiko Kasza (Scott Foresman, 1992)

Mother, Mother, I Want Another by Marie Poluskin (Crown, 1978)

The Runaway Bunny by Margaret Wise Brown (HarperCollins, 1972)

Two Other Mothers

There are some mothers that belong to everyone!

* Mother Goose is one of the most popular of all children's entertainers. Many generations of children have loved her books and stories.

* Nature is sometimes known as Mother Earth, or Mother Nature.

Recipe

Sweetheart Fudge

This delectable confection is fun for children to make and give as a gift.

※ 6 ounces milk chocolate chips

※ 12 ounces semi-sweet chocolate chips

※ 1 can sweetened condensed milk

※ 1 teaspoon vanilla

※ 1/4 cup English toffee bits

1. Melt chips and milk in microwave for two to three minutes.

2. Add vanilla to the chocolate mixture and stir well.

3. Pour the mixture into an 8-inch square pan lined with plastic wrap and sprinkle the toffee bits on top.

4. Chill for two hours. Cut into squares. Makes 36 pieces.

Mom's Stained Glass

Children can make special, personalized window decorations.

1. Children will need waxed paper (two sheets the same size), crayons, plastic knives, and flat items such as dried leaves, flower petals, stickers, glitter, confetti, paper scraps, photos (of themselves or their family), or small pictures cut from magazines.

2. Have each child choose the items he or she wants to encase in the waxed paper, and then arrange the objects on one sheet. They can then add crayon shavings or glitter for color accents (scrape wax off crayons with plastic knives).

3. (For adults only.) Put a few layers of newspaper on an ironing board. Place the waxed paper arrangement on top of this, then put the second piece of waxed paper on top of the artwork. Place a layer of newspaper on top of the whole thing. Iron on medium heat, until layers are sealed together and crayon shavings are melted.

4. Let cool and trim the edges with pinking shears.

M Is for Mother

A mother sheep is a ewe, a mother deer is a doe, and a mother horse is a mare. What names do children have for their mothers? (*Mama, Mom, Ma, Mommy, Mother*) Make a list on chart paper. Point out that all of the names begin with M. Does anyone know how to say "mother" in another language? (*madre* in Spanish, *mitera* in Greek, *ima* in Hebrew, *mere* in French). Ask, *Who has an M in his or her name?*

My Hands Can

Young children use their sense of touch extensively to explore and learn about the world around them. The activities in this theme help sharpen children's sense of touch, as well as helping them see how many things their hands can do!

Fingerplays

This week is the perfect time for "Where Is Thumbkin?" and any other fingerplays children enjoy. A great source is **http://songsfor teaching.net/fingerplays.htm**

Gingerbread Hands

Make a batch of gingerbread dough (see pages 66 and 68) and have children use a toothpick to trace each other's hands on the rolled-out dough. Cut out the hands and decorate them with raisins, sunflower seeds, sliced almonds, chocolate chips, and small candies for fingernails, rings, knuckles, and bracelets. Then bake and eat!

Your Hands Can

Then, help children practice fine-motor skills with a "My Hands Can" table. Set out small manipulative toys; button, snap, and zipper dolls; lacing boards; wooden puzzles; linking blocks; beads and string for threading; and a Feely Box (see page 107). Let children experiment with the items and discover all the things their hands can do.

Change the items on the table periodically to keep it interesting and challenging.

Talking Hands

Continue to expand children's knowledge about hands.

✳ Do children know that hands can talk? *What does it mean when someone claps their hands or snaps their fingers? What are your hands saying when you wave to a friend?*

✳ Explain that people with hearing impairments communicate with their hands, and people who do not see well read with their hands. Contact your state Board of Education for a free sample of Braille for children to explore. Use *The Handmade Alphabet* by Laura Rankin (Dial, 1991) to show children how to spell out their names in sign language.

✳ Tell children that that each finger has a different name! Expand vocabulary by sharing the words *thumb, index* (or *pointer*) *finger, middle finger, ring finger, pinky.*

✳ Expand vocabulary by making a list on chart paper of verbs that describe things hands can do (*grasp, rub, clap, snap, wipe, push, pat, roll, pinch, fold, scratch,* and so on).

✳ Tell children that each of our hands has 27 bones!

Bright Chalk Paint

Let children put their hands to work making this vividly colored paint. It's also a great way to use up little pieces of chalk!

✳ 2 tablespoons crushed chalk (have children put chalk pieces in plastic self-sealing bags, and crush them with a rolling pin until very fine)

✳ 2 tablespoons water

✳ 2 tablespoons white glue

✳ food coloring

Mix ingredients together until the mixture is a paint-like consistency. If you want fingerpaint, add less water. Use paint on dark paper or on the blacktop outdoors. Makes 1/4 cup paint.

More Feely Box Fun

Here are more activities to use with a Feely Box (see page 107).

✳ Place two items in the box, such as a small stuffed animal and a wooden block. Together with the child, place your hand in the box to help guide an item to the child's hand. Ask: *What does this feel like? Try to tell me what it is by just touching it, without using your eyes.* You can also use more challenging items, such as a pine cone, a piece of carpet, a golf ball, a baby's sock, and so on. Challenge children to name each item in the box without peeking.

✳ Play a cooperative game. Have two children each put one hand in the box. Then give the pair directions to follow using only their sense of touch, for example: *Chris, find all the smooth things and pass them to Ryan to take out of the box. Ryan, find all the rough things and pass them to Chris.* You can even incorporate counting with directions such as: *McKenzie, pass three acorns to Emily. Emily, pass four marbles to McKenzie.*

Keep these books handy all week!

Hand, Hand, Fingers, Thumb by Al Perkins (Random House, 1969)

Hand Rhymes by Marc Brown (Dutton, 1985)

My Hands by Aliki (Crowell, 1990)

My Hands Can by Jean Halzenthaler (Dutton, 1978)

Simple Signs by Cindy Wheeler (Viking, 1995)

Heavy Hands

Fill old plastic gloves with different materials (flour, playdough, dry rice, lentils, sand, and so on) and tie up with a twist-tie. Put out a few small piles of the chosen materials on a tray. Pass around the gloves one at a time and have children guess what is in each.

Clay Hands

Set out some clay and let little hands go to work! Children can pound it, poke it, pinch it, and roll it smooth. Invite them to make a pancake, a ball, a face, or a snake.

To make a clay handprint, roll clay a half-inch thick on a piece of cardboard covered with plastic wrap. The resulting shape should be round. Then help each child press an open hand into the clay to make a print. Use a toothpick to print the child's name and the date and let air dry one week. Then turn the handprints over and air dry the back for one to two days. Let children paint or shellac their prints for long-lasting keepsakes.

"My Hands Can" Pretzels

* 1 package dry yeast
* 1 1/4 cups water
* 1/2 teaspoon sugar
* 4 cups flour
* 1 teaspoon salt

Baking soda glaze:

* 1/4 cup warm water
* 1 tablespoon baking soda

1. Mix yeast, water, and sugar together in large mixing bowl and let sit for five minutes.

2. Add flour and salt and mix with a wooden spoon until well combined.

3. Turn the dough onto a floured board and knead until smooth and elastic, adding a little more flour if necessary. Let the dough rise, covered, for an hour.

4. Punch down the dough and divide into 24 pieces. Encourage children to be creative in shaping their pretzels. Show them how to use the palm of their hand to roll the dough into a rope. They can then shape the ropes into squiggles, letters, numbers, hearts, or logs. Children can also simply pound it flat with their fists, creating pretzel pizzas!

5. Place the pretzels on an greased baking sheet. Mix the baking soda glaze ingredients and let children brush it on their pretzels. You can also provide children with a variety of toppings to sprinkle on the pretzels, such as salt, cinnamon sugar, pizza spices, parmesan cheese, onion soup mix, and chocolate or colored sprinkles.

6. Let the pretzels rise for about 20 minutes and then bake at 425°F for 8 to 12 minutes, until golden. Makes 24 pretzels.

Hanimals

What else can our hands do? Find out with two imaginative books by Mario Mariotti: *Hanimals* (Simon & Schuster, 1990) and *Hanimations* (Kane Miller, 1989).

Let children try their hands at shaping some hanimals of their own. Children can use face paint (see page 149) on their hands to add a mouth or eyes, stripes or spots. Very young children will enjoy moving their hanimals and making animal sounds, while older children will enjoy weaving whole hanimal stories and putting on a hand puppet show.

Bodies in Motion

Children love to explore the many things their bodies can do, such as hop, skip, run, throw, and bat. As children play, keep in mind that actions such as hopping and skipping require muscle strength, balance, and coordination, and be prepared to modify games for children as necessary. These are designed to be fun and cooperative in spirit, making each and every child a winner!

Challenge children to try jumping backward, hopping on one foot, or holding hands with a friend and jumping together. All build coordination and gross motor skills.

Hop Like a Bunny

Rabbits have powerful back legs for hopping! Children love hopping down this bunny trail.

1. Show children how to make large hops by squatting down low and pushing off from their toes, or small hops by standing upright and bouncing on their toes.

2. When children are familiar with the action, create a bunny trail by placing carpet squares or masking tape trail markers on the floor. Position the trail markers 6 to 10 feet apart, allowing for plenty of hopping space in between. (If weather permits, you can also play this game outside: make the trail markers by sprinkling white flour on the grass.)

3. Play lively music and let the hopping begin! Show children how to hop from one carpet square or trail marker to the next, and let them pick a cut-paper carrot, lettuce, or pea pod from a basket each time they hop around the bunny trail.

Skip to My Lou

Introduce skipping or reacquaint children with this lively hop by teaching them to slowly step and then hop, first on one foot, then on the other. To help children with the mechanics of skipping, sing the tune for *Skip to My Lou*, replacing all the words with repetitions of the phrase *step hop, step hop, step hop.*

You can make a game out of *Skip to My Lou* by inviting children to skip to different objects in your classroom or play yard. Simply substitute the name of the object for the words *my Lou*, for example: *skip, skip, skip to the swings.* Or, help children practice following directions by substituting phrases such as *skip, skip, skip very fast.*

Wonderful Wiffles®

Get large muscle groups moving with a few dozen Wiffle® balls. Children can roll them, throw them, chase them, or toss them in a parachute.

To give children practice batting, hang several Wiffle® balls from a tree or piece of playground equipment with heavy string at children's chest height. (Space the balls far enough apart so that they won't get tangled or hit other children.) Invite children to bat the balls with their hands. When they have become familiar with the batting motion, let them try it with a foam bat, then with a plastic bat.

Knock It Down!

This is a simple game that children adore.

Have children stack lightweight objects, such as a set of empty frozen juice containers, film canisters, milk cartons, or tissue boxes to make a tower. Then invite children to knock it down by standing back and rolling a tennis ball toward it.

Remind children to knock down only their own towers, not the ones that someone else built! (Some children may not want to knock down their towers—that's okay too!)

More About Physical Education

❋ When children play semi-structured movement games, they improve cooperation and problem-solving skills as well as self-esteem, body awareness, and motor coordination.

❋ One of the joys of working with young children is the opportunity to let out the child in yourself! So go ahead—skip, hop, and bat along with children. They'll enjoy seeing your enthusiastic participation!

❋ Build some of these games into your regular program, giving children repeated opportunities to master them. In a few months, you'll see some big changes—and some very proud children!

❋ For more activity ideas, see *Active Learning for Fours* by Debby Cryer et al., (Addison Wesley, 1988).

❋ There's an important difference between outcome-based games, in which certain children "win" and cooperative-based games, in which children work together. When children are competing with themselves rather than against each other, they build self-esteem and develop group skills. Everyone can be a winner!

❋ For four-year-olds, movement games are a huge part of cognitive development. Children are not only building gross motor skills, they are following directions, building vocabulary, focusing their attention, sharing, developing concepts of left and right, building spatial awareness, and much more.

Take time out for some good books!

Animal Action ABC by Karen Pandell (Dutton, 1996)

Bearobics by Vic Parker (Viking, 1997)

Jiggle, Wiggle, Prance by Sally Noll (Greenwillow, 1987)

Jump, Frog, Jump! by Robert Kalan (William Morrow, 1995)

Jump Like a Frog by Kate Burns (Sterling, 1999)

Mama Zooms by Jane Cowen-Fletcher (Scholastic, 1993)

My Feet by Aliki (Crowell, 1990)

Silly Sally by Audrey Wood (Harcourt, 1994)

Teddy Bear, Teddy Bear, Turn Around by Penny Dann (Barrons, 2001)

Creepy Crawlies

One memorable June, the children in my group witnessed one of nature's miracles. I had purchased four praying mantis egg cases, and by the end of the month, nearly 600 hatchlings had emerged. The children watched the process intently, fascinated by the tiny, translucent babies. A few weeks later, 30 praying mantises remained in our garden. Now they were green, two-inch-long adolescents. The children looked for them in the garden each day, and brought them rose bush leaves for breakfast.

By the end of the summer, we had six adult praying mantises measuring five to six inches long in our yard. We watched them, and saw them watching us! We learned firsthand about how they hunt for bumblebees. We were even fortunate enough to spot one laying her eggs in September! When we cut back the garden in the late fall, we took the egg case inside and kept it safe in our refrigerator until the next year. In June, we brought it back outside and tied it to a low tree branch—and watched the process begin all over again.

Backyard Beasts

Young children are naturally fascinated by the world around them, especially living things. Whether it's a cow, bird, or ant, animals simply capture children's interest. A simple pill bug will often hold young children spellbound. Place the bug in the lid of a box, and when it begins to crawl, give it a nudge. Children will be intrigued as they see it curl up and roll like a marble. Then take children out to the yard and let them try being roly-polies themselves. Or, after a morning of observing ants scurry about as they build their anthills, encourage children to dig some anthills of their own at the sand table.

Children's curiosity makes them natural scientists as they continually investigate, explore, ask questions, and make their own discoveries. You don't have to be an entomologist to make bugs a part of your curriculum. Simply encourage children's innate interest by asking open-ended questions, even if you don't know the answers. Let children develop their own theories as to why, when, where, and what. Keep an insect identification book and magnifying glass handy throughout the summer. As children spot insects, ask: *What kind of beetle or butterfly could that be?* Call attention to body parts: *How many legs or wings does the ladybug have? Do you see the butterfly's antennae?* Make lists of what children observe, for instance, *Bugs We Saw This Week* or *Bugs With Six Legs.* Write down where children found them and what they were doing. Follow children's interests and cues: if they have lots of ant questions after discovering an ant colony, it's time for a trip to the library to find an informative book on ants.

As children explore the insect world, they not only become scientists, but they also begin to develop respect and caring for all living things—no matter how tiny!

Bug Bonanza

Insects are the most diverse, colorful, and numerous creatures on earth—and you don't have to go on a field trip to observe them! The preschool years are a wonderful time to introduce children to the world of mini-beasts, right outside your door.

Make a Bug Box

Make a safe, temporary home for an insect.

1. You will need a cylindrical oatmeal container, a sheer nylon stocking, and a pipe cleaner. Remove the lid and cut two windows out of the sides of the container.

2. Have children help you slide the container inside the stocking leg, all the way down to the toe. Cut the stocking off two to three inches above the top of the box. Then roll down the stocking and tape the edges inside the box.

3. Poke two holes in the lid and fasten the pipe cleaner to form a handle. Replace the lid.

4. Go outdoors to find your insect! Gently place the insect inside the container with a leaf and a few droplets of water. After a few hours of observation, go outside with children to return the bug to its natural habitat.

"Croak," Said the Frog

Try this froggy chant!

Croak, said the frog
*(have children make
croaking sounds)*

With his golden eyes
*(hold hands like eyeglasses
to eyes)*

Sitting on a lily pad
*(put arms in front of body to
make a round lily pad)*

Catching flies
(stick tongue out)

I have a sticky tongue as
fast as can be
(move tongue fast)

I catch mosquitoes—1, 2, 3!
*(hold up three fingers,
one at a time)*

Butterfly Symmetry

Butterflies are a perfect example of symmetry in nature. Show children photographs and drawings of butterflies. Point out that butterflies have matching patterns on their wings. Then let children experiment with symmetry themselves.

1. Cut large butterfly shapes from paper, one for each child.

2. Crease each paper butterfly down the center. Then let children dab one of the butterfly wings with several different colors of tempera paint.

3. While the paint is still wet, help children fold the other wing on top of the wet paint and press. Open the butterfly, and children will see two identical wings.

4. When dry, glue the butterflies to craft sticks. Let children "fly" their butterflies around the yard, pretending to collect nectar from flowers.

Raising Creepy Crawlies

Would you like to start an ant farm or raise your own butterflies, praying mantises, or ladybugs? Here are some companies that sell kits for raising insects:

Carolina Biological (800) 547-1733

Insect Lore (800) LIVE-BUG

Monarch Watch (785) 864-4441

Lucky Ladybugs

Children love playing with these ladybug puppets and moving the wings to make them fly.

1. For each child, set out two six-inch paper plates, red and black paint and brushes, a cork, a three-inch black paper circle, a pipe cleaner, and a paper fastener.

2. Let children paint their plates, painting one plate red and the other plate the color of their choice. When dry, cut the red plate in half. (These will become the ladybug's wings.)

3. Let children make spots on the wings with a cork dipped in black paint. Then place the wings on top of the whole plate, overlapping the upper portion of the wings, and insert the paper fastener a half inch from the edge of the plate. Before fastening, slide the black circle onto the back of the paper fastener, leaving about two-thirds of it showing for the bug's head.

4. Create a handle for the puppet by poking two holes on opposite edges of the bottom plate and stringing the pipe cleaner through. Then poke two holes in the head of the ladybug and insert smaller pieces of pipe cleaner to make antennae. You can even glue on six paper legs for a very realistic ladybug!

Check out this swarm of insect books!

Bugs by Nancy Winslow Parker (Greenwillow, 1987)

Bugs! Bugs! Bugs! by Bob Barner (Chronicle, 1999)

Flit, Flutter, Fly: Poems About Bugs and Other Crawly Creatures by Lee Bennett Hopkins (Doubleday, 1992)

The Grouchy Ladybug by Eric Carle (HarperCollins, 1977)

The Icky Bug Counting Book by Jerry Pallotta (Charlesbridge, 1992)

The Ladybug and Other Insects: A First Discovery Book by Pascale de Bourgoing (Scholastic, 1999)

Miss Spider's Tea Party by Donald Kirk (Scholastic, 1994)

Peterson's First Guide to Insects by Roger Tory Peterson (Houghton Mifflin, 1998)

The Very Hungry Caterpillar by Eric Carle (Philomel, 1969)

The Very Quiet Cricket by Eric Carle (Philomel, 1990)

Waiting for Wings by Lois Ehlert (Harcourt, 2001)

Yummy Buggies

Children can assemble their own buggy treats.

Apple Ladybugs

Use half an apple (sliced top to bottom) for body. Press on raisins for spots, using peanut butter for glue. Check for food allergies before using peanut butter. With a toothpick, attach a marshmallow for the head, then add licorice for antennae.

Spider Crackers

Spread soft cheese or peanut butter on a round cracker for body. Add eight pretzel stick legs and raisins or chocolate chips for eyes.

Ants on a Stump

Enjoy this twist on an old favorite, ants on a log! Invite children to spread peanut butter on rice cakes, then sprinkle with raisins.

Buggy Art

Here are two fun art projects to enhance your creepy-crawly theme.

* For a musical bumblebee project, cut a large bumblebee shape from fingerpaint paper for each child. Borrow a recording of Rimsky-Korsakov's *Flight of the Bumblebee* from the library, and play it as children use fingerpaint to decorate their bumblebees. *What does the music sound like to you?* Children will enjoy moving their fingers to this very lively piece of music.

* Paint with a flyswatter! Go outside and tape a large sheet of butcher paper onto a wall or fence. Pour washable paint into a shallow pan and let one or two children at a time dip flyswatters into the paint and then swat the paint onto the paper. Try using different colors, or a variety of flyswatters with different patterns.

The Woolly Caterpillar

Children will enjoy acting out this traditional chant again and again.

Little Arabella Miller
Found a woolly caterpillar.
(cup two hands together)

First it crawled upon her mother,
(walk fingers of right hand up left arm)

Then upon her baby brother.
(walk fingers of left hand up right arm)

Little Arabella Miller,
Take away the caterpillar!
(quickly move both hands behind back)

The Circus

The circus theme builds on children's natural interest in animals and creative movement. This week, transform your classroom or backyard into a circus ring complete with a tent, clowns, lions and tigers, tightrope-walkers, and even a popcorn stand! Children love to clown around and do their own "tricks," plus this theme adds plenty of color to your week.

Raise the Tent!

Here's a quick and easy way to make an indoor or outdoor big top for this theme's circus activities.

For an indoor tent, use a loop of duct tape (sticky side out) to attach the center of a colorful sheet or large parachute to your classroom ceiling. Then tie string or ribbon to each of the four corners of the sheet and secure them with duct tape to the walls of your room. Decorate your tent with streamers and balloons.

You can also simply make a circle on the floor with any combination of masking tape, ribbon, chairs, blocks, and carpet squares. (Outdoors, you can make a circus ring by sprinkling a circle of flour on the grass.)

When your circus tent and ring are complete, invite children to play animal charades. Ask children to think of an animal that they would like to be, and to keep the choice a secret. One at a time, have children go to the center of the ring and act out their animals as the group guesses.

Recipe

Face Paint

This is inexpensive and easy to make.

- 2 teaspoons cornstarch
- 3/4 teaspoon water
- 1/2 teaspoon facial cold cream
- food coloring

1. Mix cornstarch, water, and cold cream together.
2. Place the mixture in the cups of a mini-muffin tin.
3. Leave one cup of paint white and add a drop of food coloring to the others. Let children stir the mixtures with cotton swabs to blend.
4. Use cotton swabs or fingers to apply the paint. Remove with warm water.

Clowning Around

A clown's job at the circus is to get people's attention and to make them laugh. How would children like to be clowns?

Invite children to dress up as a troupe of funny clowns. Create a prop box with large t-shirts, pajama tops and bottoms, rubber noses, wigs, hats, gloves, beach balls, hula-hoops, bean bags, balloons, bubble solution (see page 160), and bubble wands. You can pad their costumes with shredded newspaper, clean rags, or towels. Tighten up large pant legs and waists by grabbing a handful of the extra fabric and securing it with a rubber band or string.

For the finishing touch, paint children's faces (see left). Children might enjoy decorating their own faces with the help of a mirror. Show children some clown faces in a book for inspiration.

Let each child have a turn. If children need help getting started, you might suggest tumbling or making funny faces. At pick-up time, have a performance for parents and caregivers!

Tightrope Walkers

Help children develop balance! Walking a tightrope requires great concentration, even if the rope is on the ground.

Set out a garden hose or thick rope and let children practice walking across it. Show them how to help steady each other by lending a hand or a shoulder. You can even have children hold cardboard wrapping paper tubes as balancing poles.

June

Recipe

Popcorn Balls

What's a circus without popcorn? An adult needs to do the first two steps of this recipe, but children love the mixing and rolling.

* 1/2 cup honey
* 1/2 cup water
* 1/3 cup butter
* 2 tablespoons vanilla
* 1/2 teaspoon salt
* 1 tablespoon wheat germ
* 5 cups popped popcorn
* 1 cup sunflower seeds
* 1 cup chopped nuts
* 1 cup raisins

1. Cook water and honey over medium heat until a candy thermometer registers 250°F (about 8 to 15 minutes). Supervise children closely for safety.

2. Remove from heat. Add butter, vanilla, salt, and wheat germ to the mixture and stir.

3. Have children mix popcorn, sunflower seeds, and nuts together in a large bowl. Pour in the first mixture and mix well.

4. Spread mixture on a baking sheet. Bake at 350°F for 20 minutes or until golden.

5. Add the raisins. While warm, children can roll into small balls, or cool and serve as is. Makes 45 one-inch balls.

Book Nook

Here are some great books to read under the big top:

Circus by Lois Ehlert (HarperCollins, 1992)

Circus by Jack Prelutsky (Macmillan, 1974)

Circus by Peter Spier (Doubleday, 1986)

The Circus Alphabet by Linda Bronson (Holt, 2001)

Olivia Saves the Circus by Ian Falconer (Atheneum, 2000)

See the Circus by H. A. Rey (Houghton Mifflin, 1998)

Spot Goes to the Circus by Eric Hill (Putnam, 1986)

Star of the Circus by Mary Beth Sampson (Holt, 1997)

The Elephant

Invite children to role-play elephants with a fun movement poem.

The elephant walks in a special way,
(sway body from side to side)

He's oh so big and oh so gray!
(spread arms wide apart)

He has no fingers,
(curl up fingers)

And you can't see his toes.

But goodness gracious, what a NOSE!
(clasp hands, straighten arms, and sway arms back and forth)

Under the Big Top

As you explore the circus theme, ask:

Have you ever been to the circus? What did you see?

Which part did you like best?

What foods did you eat? What sounds did you hear?

If you were in a circus, what job would you like to do?

Then play some music, such as Aaron Copeland's "Circus Music" from the Red Pony Ballet, and invite children to prance like ponies, plod like elephants, and lunge like lions!

More Clowning Around

Invite children to goof around and build coordination at the same time!

✳ Tape bubble wrap to the floor and have children stomp on it.

✳ Cut out child-size foot shapes from carpet. Place soft side down and have children shuffle around without losing their "clown shoes"!

✳ Stuff socks with newspaper and tie up with ribbon. Children can throw these balls indoors!

Recipe

Circus Snack

Children love creating this version of trail mix!

1. Give each child a self-sealing plastic bag and lay out ingredients and measuring cups. Invite each child to measure these amounts into his or her bag:

   ✳ 4 cups popped popcorn

   ✳ 1 cup peanuts

   ✳ 1 cup animal crackers

   ✳ 1 cup chocolate pieces (chips, candy-coated chocolate or chopped chocolate bars)

2. Then help children seal their bags and shake them up! Children can decorate their bags with stickers.

Fathers

This week, celebrate Father's Day by asking children's fathers to come in for a visit. Invite dads to share a story, meal, or activity with children. Invite each child to tell what makes his or her father special. Of course, for this week's activities, you'll want to keep in mind the diversity of family situations in your group and bring sensitivity to your planning.

Shaving Cream Fun

This tactile activity can be very soothing to children.

Squirt a ball of shaving cream for each child onto your empty sand or water table, or onto a table or trays. Add some paint or food coloring and let children squish the foam through their fingers. Ask: *How does the foam feel? Is it squishy? Silky smooth? How does it smell?*

Invite children to use their fingers to paint pictures in the shaving cream, or use it to make sculptures. They can also practice writing their names in the shaving cream. You can use different mediums for this activity. Try pudding or baby lotion on sheets of aluminum foil for easy clean-up!

Musical Shoes

Children love trying on daddy-size shoes!

Ask fathers or other male caregivers in your group to bring in a pair of their old shoes! (Have extra pairs of men's shoes available for children who are not able to bring their own.)

Help children trace the shoes onto large sheets of construction paper. Then have children set their own shoes inside the outline of their father's shoes and trace them. Help children measure the two outlines with a ruler. Ask: *Is your foot bigger or smaller than your father's? How many of your feet fit in your dad's feet? Do you think your father ever wore shoes that were your size?*

Then place all the shoes in a circle for a game of musical shoes. Turn on some music and play the game like musical chairs. When the music stops, children hop into the nearest pair of shoes! You don't need to take away any shoes each round. Kids love hopping into the shoes regardless!

Father's Day Coupons

What special things can children do for their fathers to show them how much they love them? Help children create a Father's Day card filled with "good deed" coupons that dads can redeem for special treats and favors.

1. Each child will need two sheets of colored construction paper (in different colors). Have children fold one sheet in half to make a card, then draw a portrait of their father on the front. They can also dictate a message. Add the title "Father's Day Coupons."

2. Fold the second sheet into quarters. Help children trace a hand onto the folded paper and cut through all four layers, creating four hand shapes for each child.

3. Ask children to think of four things they might do to lend a helping hand to Dad, such as give him a big hug or a foot rub, help cook dinner, weed the garden, or bring out the trash. Print one on each hand and staple the hands inside the card.

Make a Keepsake Book

For a Father's Day gift that dads will always treasure, help children create this personalized book.

Make a six-page blank book for each child. Have children decorate the covers. At the top of each page, write a sentence stem for children to complete, such as:

I love my father because...

My father's favorite food is...

My dad likes to...

When I play with my father, we like to...

The best thing about my father is...

Here's what I want to say to my dad on Father's Day:

Then page through the books with children, reading the sentence stems and asking children to complete them. Record children's dictations and then let children decorate the pages with drawings, photos, or collages.

Here are some great "Daddy" books to share.

Guess How Much I Love You by Sam McBratney (Thomas Nelson, 1999)

Happy Father's Day by Steven Kroll (Holiday House, 1988)

Just Like Daddy by Frank Asch (Prentice, 1981)

Just the Two of Us by Will Smith (Scholastic, 2001)

Messy Baby by Jan Ormerod (Walker, 1985)

Papa, Please Get the Moon for Me by Eric Carle (Simon & Schuster, 1991)

Ten, Nine, Eight by Molly Bang (Greenwillow, 1989)

Pat on the Back

Have children cover one side of a sheet of construction paper with handprints in different colors. On the other side, write *Happy Father's Day! You Deserve Lots of Pats on the Back!*

Monster Cookies

These colossal cookies are a big hit with hungry dads!

- ✳ 4 sticks butter or margarine
- ✳ 1 cup peanut or almond butter
- ✳ 1 cup brown sugar
- ✳ 1 cup white sugar
- ✳ 4 eggs
- ✳ 2 teaspoons vanilla
- ✳ 2 cups white flour
- ✳ 2 cups whole wheat flour
- ✳ 3 cups oatmeal
- ✳ 2 teaspoons baking soda
- ✳ 1 cup chopped walnuts
- ✳ 1 cup raisins
- ✳ 12 ounces chocolate chips
- ✳ 1 cup coconut flakes

Optional Toppings

Before baking, children can decorate their cookies with their choice of candy-coated chocolate, sprinkles, or miniature pretzels. After baking, they can press in big chocolate kisses or add frosting!

1. Cream together butter or margarine, nut butter, and sugar.

2. Mix in eggs and vanilla.

3. Stir in flour, oatmeal and baking soda.

4. Mix in nuts, raisins, and chips.

5. On ungreased cookie sheets, shape dough into seven large cookies, seven inches round and a half-inch thick. Use about 1 1/2 cups of dough for each cookie.

6. Sprinkle coconut on top! Bake at 375°F for 6 to 10 minutes until just beginning to brown. Makes 7 eight-inch cookies.

7. When it's time to pack up your monster cookie gifts, contact your local pizzeria for 10-inch pizza boxes! Many pizzerias will sell you the boxes for a small fee, and some might even donate them. You can cover the printing on the top of the boxes with construction paper. Print a message on each box, such as *To Dad, the Biggest Cookie for the Best Father!*

Fridge Frame

This old favorite is a perfect gift.

1. Each child will need eight craft sticks and a photo of him or herself. With tacky glue, glue the sticks together as shown. Let dry overnight.

2. Decorate the frame using paints or markers. Let dry and then decorate with sequins, buttons, construction paper, glitter, yarn, stickers, nuts and bolts, ribbons, tiny fake flowers, golf tees, puzzle pieces, lace, stamps, wrapping paper, fabric scraps, and so on.

3. Help children glue the photo to the back of the frame (trim if necessary). Add a magnetic strip so dads can proudly display on the refrigerator!

That's a Wrap!

To make special wrapping paper for gifts, have children dip the wheels of a small toy car into tempera paint. Then have them "drive" the car across a large sheet of newsprint or an opened brown paper bag. Repeat with new colors. Add car-shaped sponge prints to complete your wrapping paper.

Take Me Out to the Ball Game

Develop eye-hand coordination and reflexes in a non-competitive group game.

Read *Take Me Out To The Ball Game* by Jack Norworth (Macmillan, 1993) and teach children the song. Then bring out balls of all sizes and colors and sit in a circle with children. Have them sing the song as they roll one ball around the circle (so that each child has a turn, challenge them to roll to someone who hasn't rolled yet). Then introduce another ball and have children keep two in motion. How many balls can children keep going at once? Three? Four?

Summer Fun

Summer arrives on June 21st, the longest day of the year. The new season will bring lots of warm, sunny days for outdoor play! Talk with children about sun safety and the importance of wearing protective lotion and clothing. Remind them to drink plenty of water on hot, sunny days as well.

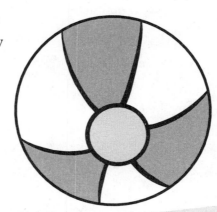

Beach Ball Bounce

For this simple summer game, you need a parachute (or large sheet cut into a circle) and a beach ball.

1. Have children stand in a circle and grip the edges of the parachute. Then toss in the beach ball. Let children create a slow wave by raising both hands up over their heads and then down to their knees, repeating the words *up* and *down* in unison.

2. Once children are comfortable with the slow wave, they can speed it up to make a fast wave or bounce. How high can children bounce it?

3. Try again with several balls, balloons, sponges, or Styrofoam eggs. How long can children keep all the items in the air?

The Beehive

Here's a poem you can use for a feltboard activity, a fingerplay, or a movement game!

Here is the beehive.
Where are the bees?
Hiding away where nobody sees.
Soon they'll be coming
Out of their hive
Let's all count them—
One, two, three, four, five.
Buzz!

For a **feltboard** activity, cut out a felt beehive (a simple oval will work fine) and five felt bees (small circles). Glue the bees onto a strip of ribbon or felt. Place the beehive on the feltboard and hide the ribbon of bees behind the hive. Then recite the poem. As you come to the last line, pull the ribbon out from behind the hive, revealing one bee at a time.

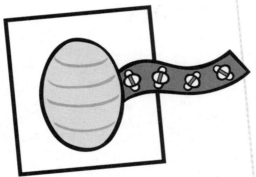

For a **fingerplay**, have children lace their fingers together to make a hive. As they count off the bees, show them how to raise the fingers of one hand, one at a time.

For a **movement** activity, let five children play bees. Have them hide under a sheet or parachute "hive." Then ask them to run out of the hive, one at a time, as you count.

Cool down with a good book!

Animals in Summer by Jane McCauley (Random House, 1994)

Counting Our Way to Maine by Maggie Smith (Orchard Books, 1995)

Good Lemonade by Frank Asch (Watts, 1976)

Mr. Gumpy's Outing by John Burningham (Holt, 1971)

The Summer Night by Charlotte Zolotow (HarperCollins, 1991)

Summersaults by Douglas Florian (Greenwillow, 2002)

Ten Flashing Fireflies by Philemon Sturges (North-South Books, 1995)

When Summer Comes by Robert Maass (Holt, 1996)

Purple Cow Smoothies

Recite this old favorite with children, then make your own purple cows!

I never saw a purple cow,
I never hope to see one.
But I can tell you anyhow,
I'd rather see than *be* one!

Ask children: *Have you ever seen a purple cow? What would you do if you saw one? Have you ever seen purple milk? Where does milk come from?*

Then whip up a batch of Purple Cows! This is a smooth, refreshing summer drink that children love not only for the taste and color, but also for the whimsical poem that inspired it.

* 1/3 cup grape juice concentrate
* 1 frozen ripe banana, cut into chunks
* 3 heaping tablespoons non-fat powdered milk
* 3/4 cup milk
* 1 1/2 cups vanilla ice cream or frozen yogurt

1. Blend the juice and banana in food processor or blender (supervise children closely).

2. Dissolve the powdered milk in the liquid milk and add to blender.

3. Add ice cream or yogurt and blend. Makes six 1/2 cup servings.

The addition of non-fat dry milk gives this smoothie an extra boost of calcium, making it a healthy snack or dessert. You can also fill half-cup containers with the smoothie and place them in the freezer. In a few hours you'll have ice cream!

Gardens Are for Eating!

If you started a garden this spring, the fruits, vegetables, and herbs should be starting to sprout. Part of summer fun is being able to pick and eat your sun-warmed bounty. Show children which plants are safe to pick and eat. Remind them to wash fruits, vegetables, and herbs before eating, and to stay away from harmful plants such as holly berries, wild mushrooms, or poison ivy.

Ice Rainbow

This colorful activity will cool children off on a hot summer day.

Fill six ice cube trays with water, add a different food coloring to each tray, and freeze. Fill your water table or a large plastic tub with water. Then let children play with different color combinations of ice cubes in the water. As they play, ask: *What do you think is going to happen to the ice cubes? How is the color of the water changing?*

For more icy fun, make ice cubes from different kinds of juice (orange, cranberry apple, grape, lemonade) and add to water or club soda. *How do the colors change?* Or, sprinkle several colors of powdered tempera paint on paper and have children "paint," using ice cubes as brushes.

Best Bubbles

This inexpensive bubble solution yields bigger, sturdier bubbles than commercial solutions.

Mix one part dishwashing liquid with two parts water and let sit overnight (allowing the mixture to "rest" for at least 12 hours will give the solution a nice thick consistency). Add a few drops of glycerin (available at drugstores).

If you mix a quart bottle of dishwashing liquid with two quarts of water and store it in a gallon container, you will have enough bubble solution to last for months!

Bubble-Blowing Fun

Improvise different bubble-blowers for children to use. Try using a small paper cup with holes punched in the bottom, a bundle of straws held together with a rubber band, or a plastic strawberry basket. Children can even be the bubble-blowers themselves! Show them how to make an O with their thumb and forefinger, dip the O in bubble solution, and blow!

Lemonade Play Dough

Start your summer with a new batch of lemony play dough. This dough smells great and will stay fresh in the refrigerator for up to two months.

* ❋ 2 1/2 cups flour
* ❋ 1/2 cup salt
* ❋ 3 packs unsweetened lemonade drink mix
* ❋ 3 tablespoons oil
* ❋ 2 cups boiling water

Mix the salt, flour, and drink mix together. Then mix in the oil and boiling water (adult only). Cool the dough slightly and let children knead it until smooth. Makes 3 cups.

Good Lemonade

Welcome the summer season by letting children squeeze lemons, grate rind, and experience the difference between sweet and sour as they make real lemonade. Let children take turns squeezing the lemons on a citrus reamer. For safety, watch children's knuckles when grating rind and make sure an adult takes over when it's time to add the boiling water.

* ❋ 1 tablespoon grated lemon rind
* ❋ fresh-squeezed juice of 9 lemons
* ❋ 5 cups cold water
* ❋ 1/2 cup boiling water
* ❋ 1 1/2 cups sugar

1. Combine the rind, juice, and cold water and set aside.

2. Combine the boiling water and sugar and stir into first mixture.

3. Serve over ice. Garnish with lemon and orange slices and fresh mint. Makes 7 eight-ounce cups.

Creative Recycling

As you know, running an early childhood classroom or center can be expensive. If there's one surefire way to keep expenses down, it's to turn a creative eye towards the items you already own—and on "trash" that's headed for the garbage can! Art supplies abound in most households, disguised in many forms, and it only takes a little creativity to recycle them into useful materials for hours of learning and fun.

In my own room, the art supply shelf looks more like a recycling center, and that's exactly what it is! I save brown paper bags, newspapers, Styrofoam produce trays, egg cartons, egg shells, aluminum pie pans, milk caps, jugs, cartons, coffee cans, yogurt cups, bread bag tabs, twist ties, sawdust, dryer lint, film canisters, evergreen needles, shirt cardboards, frozen juice lids, ribbon, beads, and many other odds and ends that come my way.

You may not find all the supplies you need around your own house, but friends, relatives, and neighbors may have just what you're looking for. Distribute a list of "most wanted" items to friends and family members. You may even get bonus items you didn't ask for.

From Trash to Treasure

Yard sales and thrift shops are great resources for adding inexpensive supplies to your art shelf, but some of the very best art supplies are absolutely free, and they're available to anyone who asks. Check out some of these resources in your own community:

Home supply and decorating shops are often willing to donate carpet remnants and outdated wallpaper and carpet sample books.

Billboard companies (look under *Advertising–Outdoor* in the yellow pages) often give away giant sheets of sturdy, folded billboard paper that have been cut or printed incorrectly, or are simply left over. These sheets are usually white on one side with sections of print and bright colors on the other. Their size and durability make them perfect for children's murals and display boards. They can also be used as drop cloths under a painting or craft area. Newspaper printing companies also have reams of roll-ends (rolls of blank newsprint paper too small for their presses) that will last you for months.

Cardboard boxes make versatile supplies for art projects, as well as storage. Boxes of every size and shape are only as far away as your nearest store. At the supermarket you can find egg cases and banana boxes. Stationery and book stores have sturdy medium-size cartons. You can find extra-large boxes at appliance stores. There are a multitude of uses for refrigerator boxes (you'll find many ideas throughout this book, including puppet theaters, trains, and castles). Get to know local store managers; they are usually quite willing to give surplus boxes a good home! A grocery store manager once called to tell me he was throwing out a colorful animal cracker display box. We got about three months of heavy use out of it!

Once you begin to look at common items with a creative eye, it's possible to implement a diverse, creative curriculum with recycled materials. With a little glue, paint, glitter, and markers, children can turn "trash" into treasure!

Red, White & Blue

Everyone loves a birthday party, and on the Fourth of July our country has one! Hang a U.S. map and show children the 50 states that make up our country. Help children find their state, and ask if anyone has friends or relatives in different states. Explain that each state also has a star on the American flag. Invite them to say *Happy Birthday, America!*

Handprint Flag

Here is a simple, hands-on way to celebrate the stars and stripes.

1. Set out a large sheet of white mural paper, or a white sheet and fabric paints. Glue a large square of blue paper or fabric onto the upper left corner of the flag, or paint blue and let dry.

2. Let children dip their hands into shallow containers of white tempera paint and press them onto the blue square. Can you fit exactly fifty?

3. Next, have children dip clean hands into red paint to print stripes across the flag.

Uncle Sam Hats

Children can make their own party hats.

1. Give each child a white nine-inch paper plate with the center cut out. Provide children with star-shaped sponges and dishes of red and blue paint, as well as markers, crayons, and bingo bottles (see page 75).

2. Have children use the sponge-paints and other materials to decorate the paper plate rim. Then have them decorate large sheets of white construction paper.

3. When dry, roll the sheet of paper into a tube so that it fills the opening in the paper plate. Then remove the tube and tape it shut. Cut one-inch slits around the bottom of the paper tube to create tabs, and insert the tube back into the paper plate opening.

4. Then fold up the tabs and tape them to the bottom of the paper plate rim to secure. Punch a hole in each side of the plate, knot a piece of string in each hole, and tie the hats under children's chins.

Book Nook

Celebrate America with a good book!

America the Beautiful by Katherine Bates (Atheneum, 1993)

Apple Pie, Fourth of July by Janet S. Wong (Harcourt, 2002)

Hats Off for the Fourth of July by Harriet Ziefert (Viking, 2000)

Henry's Fourth of July by Holly Keller (Greenwillow, 1985)

Hurray for the Fourth of July by Wendy Watson (Clarion, 1992)

Parade by Donald Crews (Greenwillow, 1986)

This Land Is Your Land by Woody Guthrie (Little Brown, 1998)

Splatter a Star

Cut out large paper stars, one per child. Spread newspaper over the work surface and have children use paintbrushes, toothbrushes, or old feather dusters to splatter them with red, white, and blue paint.

Recipe

Red, White & Blue Sundaes

Have a birthday party for America with these festive treats.

Set out a buffet of blueberries, sliced raspberries or strawberries, vanilla yogurt, and whipped cream. Place each item in a separate bowl. Then give children small bowls and spoons and invite them to create their own sundaes. Or give each child a small bowl of vanilla yogurt or pudding and put one drop of red, and one drop of blue, food coloring on top. Children love to mix it up to make purple!

Red, White & Blue Beads

Children will enjoy working with dyed pasta to create patriotic necklaces and bracelets.

Pour three cups of rubbing alcohol into a container with a tight-fitting lid. Add three tablespoon of red food coloring and a box of tubular pasta, such as ziti or rigatoni. In a separate container, create the same solution using blue food coloring, again adding a box of pasta. (Supervise children closely for safety near rubbing alcohol.) Cover the container for three to six hours, stirring often. Use a box of pasta (undyed) for white beads.

When the pasta is dyed, spread it out on paper towels to dry. Then let children string their red, white, and blue beads on yarn to make necklaces and bracelets. If you make a large batch of dyed pasta, children can string patriotic garlands for decorating stair railings, mantels, doorways, and trees.

I Love a Parade!

Play patriotic music and have a parade! Invite children to put on their beads (see above) and Uncle Sam hats (see page 164), grab their noisemakers (see page 166), and march around the classroom or yard. You might also decorate trikes and riding toys with red, white, and blue streamers and have a bike rally.

Yankee Doodle Noisemakers

Yankee Doodle stuck a feather in his hat and called it macaroni! Invite children to make noisemakers of their own.

Make yankee doodle maracas! Give each child two paper plates and a handful of dried small elbow pasta. Have children put the pasta on one paper plate (bottom side down), then place the other plate on top of the first plate (bottom side up). Staple their plates together (with pasta inside), let dry, and have children decorate with glue, glitter, stickers, and markers. Bring them along on a parade!

Frozen Fun!

It's July and the temperature is rising! Add to the Fourth's festivities with these cooling and nutritious pops.

Prepare packages of both red and blue jello. When cooled but still liquid, have children whisk in a half cup of vanilla yogurt. Pour into small paper cups (first the red, then the blue, so that the result is half red and half blue), add a craft stick, and freeze until firm. Let children peel off the paper cups and enjoy their homemade treats.

Fireworks

Discuss the beautiful patterns and colors fireworks make against the night sky and then let children make their own firework designs. Here are four different ways:

❋ Have children drizzle and drip slightly thinned white glue from the end of a Popsicle stick onto a piece of black paper. Then let them sprinkle colored glitter over the glue. You might play patriotic music as children work on their designs.

❋ Put large drops of blue and red tempera paint on white paper. Then have children blow on them with straws to create little fireworks.

❋ For each child, draw a large firework on black construction paper with chalk. Have children "trace" over them using squeeze-top glue. Then have them ball up one-inch squares of colored tissue paper, one at a time, and place them on the glue.

❋ Paint the entire surface of the a sheet of white cardboard with thinned white glue. Fill shakers with powdered tempera and glitter and shake onto the glue to create fireworks. Let dry for several days.

Working With Wood

Wood is a wonderfully tactile medium, and it's a material found all around us. Plus, many children are fascinated with construction and construction workers! Young children can learn to work safely with wood and tools if you gradually introduce woodworking skills and safety precautions, and give children practice, guidelines, and close supervision. Working with wood will build coordination, concentration, and basic mechanical understanding of tools and materials.

Why Wood?

Children love the feel of tools and the smell of fresh sawdust. Woodworking appeals to their senses and creative urges, and also develops fine-motor control, muscle strength, and eye-hand coordination. When woodworking with children, remember that the value is always in the process, not the product. Of course, check that wood is splinter-free and model responsible use of tools.

Wood, Wood, Wood

Set out a collection of wood pieces in as many different types, sizes, and forms as possible. Include soft woods such as pine and balsam and hard woods such as oak and maple, as well as craft sticks, wooden spools, wooden bowls, scraps of plywood, a log, a wooden crate, and so on. (Be sure to check each piece of wood first, making sure it is safe for children to handle.)

Let children touch the wood, smell it, stack it, and sort it. Ask: *Where does wood come from? What do we use wood for?* (pencils, paper, books, homes, toys, and so on) List children's ideas on chart paper. If possible, follow up with a visit to a lumberyard!

Starting Out

Use safety tools so children can practice woodworking skills as they build coordination in a safe environment.

✳ Show children a set of "grown-up" tools: hammers, saws, screwdrivers, pliers, sanding blocks, files, nails, screws, vises, and so on. Teach children what each tool is for and how it is used.

✳ Young children can get lots of practice with plastic hammers. Give them small balls of clay to flatten. Children can also use carpenter's glue until they are ready for other tools. Offer them a variety of wood pieces of different shapes and sizes for building freeform structures.

✳ Styrofoam packing pieces (available free from appliance stores) and golf tees make great make-believe wood and nails. Children can build constructions by joining two or more pieces of foam together using golf tees and a plastic hammer or wooden mallet. Styrofoam can also be "sawed" with plastic picnic knives.

Book Nook

Build interest with books!

Building a House by Byron Barton (Greenwillow, 1981)

A Carpenter by Douglas Florian (Greenwillow, 1991)

The House I'll Build for the Wrens by Shirley Neitzel (Greenwillow, 1997)

Old MacDonald Had a Woodshop by Lisa Schulman (Putnam, 2002)

The Toolbox by Anne & Harlow Rockwell (Macmillan, 1971)

Who Builds? by Michael Rex (HarperCollins, 1999)

Woodworking for Kids by Kevin McGuire (Sterling, 1993)

More Woody Fun

✳ Fill your sand table with sawdust! Bury wooden blocks in the dust.

✳ Invite a carpenter to visit and talk about his or her work.

✳ Examine a tree stump for rings.

Build a Boat

Let children construct their own boats for the water table.

Set out a collection of wood pieces (be sure they are smooth enough for children to handle safely) along with wooden spools and dowels, craft sticks, bottle caps, and bits of fabric for flags and sails. Children can select wood pieces, stack them, and attach them with wood glue. Wait for glue to dry before children sand and paint their creations. Then set sail!

Carpenter's Hands

Sing this chant to introduce even the youngest toddler to the basic mechanics of woodworking. As you chant each verse, pantomime the carpenter's actions and invite children to follow.

This is the way I saw the wood,

Saw the wood, saw the wood,

This is the way I saw the wood,

Oh, so carefully.

Repeat, substituting the phrase *saw the wood* with:

Hammer the nail...

Turn the screw...

Sand it smooth...

Paint the wood...

Use a wrench...

Pour cement...

Sandpaper Fun

Many children enjoy sanding wood. It's great fine-motor and coordination practice, and a great release of extra energy! Try these sandpaper activities:

✳ Write on sandpaper with pencil.

✳ Draw on fine sandpaper with colored chalk.

✳ Try sanding off pencil writing on wood (use a block covered in sandpaper so children can easily manipulate).

✳ Set out an assortment of sandpaper in different degrees of coarseness (fine, medium, coarse). Let children feel and discuss the differences.

✳ Sand different shapes of scrap wood.

✳ Sand different types of wood with the same sandpaper block and and compare the results.

(adapted from Dr. Polly Adams and Dr. Jaynie Nesmith, "Building and Maintaining a Developmentally Appropriate Woodworking Center"; NAEYC presentation 1998)

On the Farm

Have children ever seen a pig up close, touched a woolly sheep, or heard a rooster crow? If possible, arrange a visit to a local farm, petting zoo, or county fair. By seeing, hearing, and touching the animals, children will have a chance to gather their own information about their barnyard friends. Exploring the farm theme also helps children build concepts about production and consumption. Lots of our food comes from farms!

Big Red Barn

Read Margaret Wise Brown's classic _Big Red Barn_ (HarperCollins, 1989) with children and then work together to construct a barn of your own.

Ask an appliance store to save a refrigerator box for you. Tape both ends of the box with strong tape. Cut barn doors in one side and have children paint the barn red! Then spread some clean hay inside along with toy farm animals and baskets. Invite children to invent stories with their props, or put on a barnyard show.

Mary Had a Little Lamb

Sing the farm classic, "Mary Had a Little Lamb," then have children make their own lambs!

1. Each child will need sheet of cardboard, a large adults handful of cotton balls, and two clothespins. Cut the shape of a lamb from cardboard for each child.

2. Let children draw a face and glue cotton balls to the body.

3. Attach two clothespins for legs.

Old MacDonald Had a Farm

When asked where their food comes from, many children will reply "the grocery store!" Talk with children about the real sources of milk, cheese, eggs, and other dairy products.

Cut simple farm animal and food shapes out of felt. Include a cow, a chicken, eggs, butter, milk, cheese, ice cream, and so on. Place all the pieces on a feltboard. Then sing a round of "Old MacDonald" with children. As you sing each verse, let children take turns matching the animals to the foods they produce.

Animal Fair

Have children bring their favorite stuffed animals to school for an animal fair.

Have children hold their animals at circle time. Ask the group to describe what they like best about each animal and decide what makes each one special: best eyes, best personality, softest fur, funniest, biggest, smallest, and so on. Give each animal an award sticker.

Farmhands' Overnight French Toast

Many people's mornings start just as early, and are just as busy, as mornings on a farm. With this recipe, which you put together the day before and then bake at mealtime, you can serve a hearty breakfast (or lunch) in a jiffy!

- ✳ 3 eggs
- ✳ 1 1/2 cups milk
- ✳ 2 tablespoons brown sugar
- ✳ 1 1/2 teaspoons cinnamon
- ✳ 1 teaspoon vanilla
- ✳ 1 loaf day-old Italian bread

1. Mix eggs, milk, sugar, cinnamon, and vanilla together. Place in shallow container.

2. Slice the bread into 8 one-inch thick slices.

3. Soak bread slices in the egg and milk mixture for 5 minutes on one side, then turn them over. Cover and refrigerate overnight.

4. In the morning, place the bread on a buttered cookie sheet at 400°F for 10 minutes. Turn slices over and bake 10 more minutes until golden.

5. Top with syrup or fresh fruit. Serves four to eight.

Animal Match-Ups

Share a big box of animal crackers at snack time. Have children choose their crackers by following directions such as: *Find one horse to put on your plate. Now find a pair of sheep. Find as many goats as you can. Line up three cows in a row.*

Kick back with a good book!

All About Farm Animals by Brenda Cook (Doubleday, 1988)

Barn Dance by Bill Martin Jr. & John Archambault (Holt, 1986)

Barnyard Banter by Denise Fleming (Holt, 1994)

Click, Clack, Moo: Cows That Type by Doreen Cronin (Simon & Schuster, 2000)

Country Fair by Gail Gibbons (Little Brown, 1994)

Giggle, Giggle, Quack by Doreen Cronin (Simon & Schuster, 2002)

The Milk Makers by Gail Gibbons (Little Brown, 1993)

Our Animal Friends at Maple Hill Farm by Alice & Martin Provensen (Random House, 1974)

Spots, Feathers, and Curly Tails by Nancy Tafuri (Greenwillow, 1988)

Wake Up, Farm by Alvin Tresselt (Lothrop, 1991)

Farm Magnets

Use animal crackers to make magnets. Let children paint the crackers with acrylic paints. When dry, apply a coat of clear varnish, if you wish, and glue a small magnet to the back. Line up the animals on your refrigerator or another metallic surface for a parade!

All Kinds of Farms

There are many types of farms, and farmers raise animals for different reasons. Some animals are raised for food (meat, milk, eggs) and some for other products (wool, fertilizer). Help children look around the classroom, yard, and neighborhood and make a list of the items they see that come from farm animals. Besides food, there are horsehair paint brush bristles, down pillows, wool sweaters, and more! *If you were a farmer, what sorts of animals would you have on your farm?*

Farmer's Market

Create a farmer's market in the dramatic play area.

Once children have built background knowledge about farms, they may enjoy selling their very own farm-fresh produce! Add these to the center:

* plastic fruits and vegetables
* empty, clean milk cartons
* plastic cider containers
* pie tins
* straw baskets
* plastic berry baskets
* paper bags
* play money and money box
* paper and pencil for creating price signs and adding up purchases

Visiting a Farm

Teach children the following song (sing to the tune of "Row, Row Your Boat"). Then invite them to make up their own verses with different animals and sounds.

Went to visit a farm one day,
Saw a cow across the way,
What do you think I heard it say?
Moo, moo, moo, moo, moo!

All Aboard!

What's it like to ride on a real train? If possible, let children find out by arranging a short trip on a local train, even if it's only for several stops and back again. Point out the station, the ticket booth, and the different cars. The engineers and conductors are usually happy to greet a group of young children and talk about their jobs. Even if a ride on a real train is not possible, the activities in this theme will introduce children to the fun and excitement of train travel.

Ride a Train

It's easy to make your own train! Create a dramatic play area for your little conductors, mechanics, and passengers.

1. Use a large refrigerator box. Tape closed and cut as shown at right.

2. Provide passengers with old suitcases (they're easy to find at yard sales) to fill with doll clothes or clothes from the dramatic play area. A paper bag or box with holes cut in it can serve as a pet carrier.

3. Provide the crew with caps (such as painter's caps), whistles, tickets, hole punchers for punching tickets, megaphones made from rolled-up posterboard for announcing stops, and signal lamps.

Choo-Choo

Little train enthusiasts will learn this movement chant in a flash!

Here is the train,
(make a fist)
Here is the track,
(extend other arm)
Choo choo forward,
(slide fist forward along arm)
Choo choo back.
(slide fist backward along arm)
Here are the wheels,
Going clickety-clack,
(move hands in rolling motion)
Poof goes the smoke,
(place arms over head)
From the big smoke stack!
(clap hands over head on the word "stack")

This poem is also fun to recite as children act out their own train. Line children up and have each child hold the waist of the child in front of him. Let children take turns being the engine, the freight car, the passenger car, and the caboose. Toot, toot, you're off!

Whistle While You Work

For realistic sound effects, you can buy inexpensive wooden train whistles at a toy store. To find out what different whistle signals mean, read *Train Whistles* by Helen Sattle (Lothrop, 1977). Children also love hearing you whistle!

I Think I Can

Read Watty Piper's *The Little Engine that Could* (Putnam, 1976) with children. It's a wonderful story with a message that never goes out of style. After reading, help each child think of something that takes practice to do. Then make a motivating train engine to encourage children to reach for their goals.

Cut a train engine shape from paper for each child. Have children paint their engines with bingo bottles (see page 75), sponges, or brushes. Print the phrase *I Think I Can* on the back of each engine along with the child's goals.

The Peanut

This simple fingerplay never fails to delight children.

Peanut sat on a railroad track,
Its heart was all a-flutter,
(flutter hand over heart)

Along came the five-fifteen –
(zoom hand in front of body)

Oops!
(cup hand at mouth)

Peanut butter!

Recipe

Wonder Dough

This dough has a smooth, rubbery quality that children love to work with. Let children use their Wonder Dough with train-theme cookie cutters.

✳ 9 slices of Wonderbread ™ with crusts removed

✳ 6 tablespoons white glue

✳ 1/4 teaspoon white vinegar

1. Have an adult place the bread in a food processor or blender and pulse until crumbs are formed.

2. Mix the glue and vinegar together. Add the breadcrumbs.

3. Mix well with hands until the texture is silky. (Hint: rub a dab of hand soap onto hands before mixing.)

4. Divide the dough into quarters and work a different color food coloring into each batch. Makes one cup.

Children can use the dough to create train sculptures, or roll it out and cut it with cookie cutters. Air dry the sculptures or dry them for two hours

Book Nook

All aboard for a good book!

All Aboard ABC by Doug Magee (Dutton, 1990)

Chugga Chugga Choo Choo by Kevin Lewis (Hyperion, 2001)

Freight Train by Donald Crews (Greenwillow, 1978)

Train Leaves the Station by Eve Merriam (Holt, 1992)

Trains: A First Discovery Book by Gallimard Jeunesse (Cartwheel, 1998)

Train Song by Harriet Ziefert (Scholastic, 2000)

Train Travel

Share some history with children.

✳ Before there were cars and airplanes, there were trains.

✳ People traveled from town to town and all the way across the country on trains.

✳ In the early days of train travel, it took weeks and weeks to get from coast to coast.

✳ Today, an airplane can take you from one coast of the country to the other in about five hours!

Train Talk

Get children thinking at high speed!

* *Where would you like to go by train? How long do you think it would take to get there? What would you need to bring?*

* *Have you ever taken a really long train ride, one where you actually slept overnight and ate on a train? What was it like?*

* *Would you like to be the engineer or conductor on a train? How about a waiter or chef?*

* *How do you think trains move?*

* *What do you suppose moves faster, a train or a bicycle?*

* *What types of trains can you think of? (subway, elevated, high-speed, old-fashioned)*

Recipe

Pecan Pleasers

These pack well in a tin for pretend train travel. Enjoy at snack time in the "dining car" of your backyard train!

* 1/2 cup rolled oats
* 3/4 cup brown sugar, packed
* 1 stick butter, room temperature
* 1 cup flour

Topping:

* 1 teaspoon vanilla
* 2 tablespoons flour
* 3/4 cup dark corn syrup
* 1 cup chopped pecans
* 3 eggs

1. Mix first four ingredients (oats, sugar, butter, flour) together and press into a greased 9-inch square pan. Bake at 350°F for 15 minutes.

2. Mix topping ingredients together and pour over baked crust. Bake at 350°F for 25 minutes until golden brown and set.

3. Let cool, then chill. Cut into bite-size squares.

Summertime!

Bare feet, sticky Popsicles, and sweet corn—these are vivid memories from my childhood summers. The days were long and spent outside: cloud gazing, tree climbing, playing hide-and-seek, and watching glowing fireflies at dusk. I learned how to make a blade of grass sing and how to skip a stone. I watched a wasp make its paper nest and saw cicadas molt. Summer days were about exploring and making discoveries.

Summertime is full of opportunities for children to explore, run, and play. The days are longer, and there's plenty of time to spend on seasonal pleasures such as picking strawberries, making pies, hiking a nature trail, wading in a lazy stream, or napping under a tree.

Summer Traditions

Summer is also a wonderful time to sow the seeds of tradition. A workshop speaker I once heard said, "Traditions are hooks on which children can hang their memories." The daily or weekly activities that your group participates in can become memories that each child will treasure forever.

Try introducing children to a few traditions from your own childhood, or create some new ones for children to carry on. While traditions often come from our cultural backgrounds, they can come from other, more everyday sources as well. Traditions can grow from children's own interest, or from ideas that you've gotten from other families or groups. Here are a few ideas to get going:

✳ Preschoolers love "food traditions." You might start a Wednesday-afternoon make-your-own-pizza, or ice-cream sundae tradition. Or declare every Monday "Pajama Monday" and let children wear p.j.'s and slippers as you make pancakes or waffles together. Surprise children with a different topping each week!

✳ Ask if families are interested in starting a Friday "iced tea time." At pick-up time, invite parents and caregivers to put their feet up while children serve them cool glasses of homemade sun tea. This is a great way to relax while forming a strong sense of community as well.

✳ Begin a tradition of discovery. Once or twice a month, venture out for a field trip to a new place. With an adult for every three children, you can easily and safely take your group on exploratory adventures. Try going to the beach, the town library, a nature trail, a new playground, or even a farm.

Follow the Leaders!

Listen, observe, and follow children's lead this summer as they make discoveries and find new interests. Perhaps the most important tradition you can begin with children is the tradition of lifelong learning. With your encouragement and support, their natural interest and curiosity can turn them into junior entomologists, botanists, zoologists, and earth scientists. And as children make new discoveries, they take joy in the process of discovery itself—a joy that can last a lifetime!

Sunny Days

I t's August, the sun is shining, and the weather is hot! Lots of cool summer drinks and water play will help cool everyone down. If the heat is making everyone a little sleepy, these summery activities are sure to spark children's interest and wake everyone right up!

Solar Prints

T o make sun prints, have each child place an assortment of small, flat objects (such as leaves, lace, coins, plastic letters, keys, and so on) on a piece of dark construction paper. Then leave in direct sunlight (do this for several hours over a period of a few days). What do children think will happen? Remove the objects and find out!

Commercial kits for sun prints (ones that come out more dramatically than on construction paper) are available through Educational Insights (www.edin.com).

Pick-Your-Own Potpourri

1. Go flower picking! Show children the difference between a fresh flower and a flower that is past its prime. Let them pick the fading ones. If you don't have a garden in your yard, you might ask a neighbor or the superintendent of a nearby park to donate "fading" flowers.

2. Inside, spread out each batch of flowers in a tray or shallow box and place in a sunny window. When the flowers are dried, store them in a plastic self-sealing bag. Continue collecting flowers until you have enough to make a small sachet for each child.

3. To make potpourri, gather a selection of sweet-smelling spices (such as cinnamon and cloves) and perfume. Let children have fun sniffing the different scents. Let each child choose which scent to sprinkle or spray onto the dried flowers. Then cut six-inch squares of fabric, place two to three tablespoons of potpourri on each one, and tie up with ribbon.

179

Blade Buzzer

To make a musical blade buzzer, you will need two tongue depressors, a rubber band, and a six-inch blade of crab grass (a wide piece works best). First, help children sandwich the grass between the tongue depressors. Then wrap the rubber band tightly around one end. Show children how to use one hand to hold the buzzer horizontally by the rubber-band end. Children can play the blade buzzer harmonica-style by blowing through it.

Book Nook

Find a shady spot and share a story!

Central Park Serenade by Laura Godwin (Joanna Cotler, 2002)

Cool Ali by Nancy Poydar (McElderry, 1996)

Cornfield Hide and Seek by Christine Widman (Farrar Straus & Giroux, 2003)

Marshmallow Kisses by Linda Crotta Brennan (Houghton Mifflin, 2000)

One Hot Summer Day by Nina Crews (Greenwillow, 1995)

What Can You Do in the Sun? by Anna Grossnickle Hines (Greenwillow, 1999)

Sun Safety

✳ Remind children never to look directly at the sun.

✳ Teach children how to protect themselves from the sun by playing in the shade whenever possible, wearing hats, and applying sunscreen. Sunblock comes in a variety of colors, which not only encourages children to protect their sensitive lips, noses, and cheeks, but makes fantastic face paint, too!

✳ Have water bottles for each child to tote along on summer outings. Encourage children to drink plenty of water on hot days.

✳ Try a game of shadow tag in the afternoon, when the sun is casting long shadows and the day is beginning to cool off. Shadows are fun to play in, and help protect children's skin, too.

Recipe

Bug Juice

Have children invent their own juice! Set out containers of different juices and fruit, measuring cups and spoons, and paper cups and let children go to work!

- ✳ pineapple juice
- ✳ orange juice
- ✳ cranberry juice
- ✳ grape juice
- ✳ apple juice
- ✳ canned chopped peaches
- ✳ canned pineapple chunks
- ✳ sliced strawberries
- ✳ sliced frozen bananas

Invite children to concoct their own version of bug juice using different quantities of their chosen ingredients. Record each child's recipe so he or she can try it again at home. Serve cold, or pour into ice cube trays or juice-pop molds and freeze.

Reflect It!

Children can bounce the sun's rays with homemade reflectors. Use aluminum foil to cover a paper plate, pie tin, or piece of cardboard. Hold and wiggle the foil near a sunny window to see the sunlight dance around the room (remind children to not look directly at the foil).

Sun Clocks

Explain that long ago, before there were clocks, people used the sun to tell time. They used the shadow that the sun made on a sundial—and children can make their very own!

1. All you need is a sunny day, a paper plate, and two pencils. Early in the day, take children outdoors to an open, sunny area.

2. Make a hole in the center of the plate. Insert the pencil point through the hole in the plate and then press into the ground.

3. Point out that the pencil creates a shadow. Use the other pencil to trace a line on the plate along the shadow and mark the time on the line.

4. Each hour, draw a line along the new shadow and mark the time again. By the end of the day, you will have a sun clock. Compare it to the clock indoors!

Camp Out

Camping is one of summer's most exciting pleasures. The joy of being outside, following a trail, glimpsing a deer, and falling asleep under the stars are unforgettable experiences for children. But you don't need to go to a campsite to have a camping adventure! In this theme you'll find plenty of activities that capture the fun of camping right in your own backyard or school grounds.

What's in My Backpack?

Show children an authentic, lightweight hiker's frame backpack. Children will enjoy trying it on and filling it up with camp gear. (A smaller canvas or nylon backpack will work, too.) Stock the backpack with camping essentials such as a canteen, compass, trail map, sleeping bag, flashlight, first-aid kit, an empty, clean container of bug repellent, toilet tissue, soap, towels, toothbrush, ground cloth, dish, cup, spoon, and fork. You might also include a few fun non-essentials, such as freeze-dried ice cream, a harmonica, a Frisbee, or a teddy bear.

At circle time, ask if children if they have ever gone camping. *Where did you go? What did you bring? What fun things did you do?* Then let each child reach into the backpack and remove one item. Ask: *What is it used for? Why would you need it on a camping trip?* Discuss the things that people need to survive (food, water, shelter.) Continue until the pack is empty.

Leave the backpack in the dramatic play center (you might even pitch a real tent there as well)!

Pack a Snack!

Healthy snacks that are high in energy-producing carbohydrates and low in salt are great for munching while resting on a rock or beside a stream. Here are two great snacks to take on outdoor adventures.

Recipe

Trail Mix

Children will have fun scooping, measuring, and mixing this trail mix. Give each child a sandwich-size self-sealing bag. Have each child use measuring cups to put the following in their bag:

* ⚹ 1/4 cup bran square cereal
* ⚹ 1/4 cup shredded wheat mini-squares
* ⚹ 1/4 cup round rice cereal
* ⚹ 1/4 cup O-shaped oat cereal
* ⚹ 1/4 cup puffed wheat or puffed rice
* ⚹ 1/4 cup raisins

Recipe

Fruit Leather

Invite children to make their own fruit roll-ups! While an adult must operate the blender and pour the fruit puree onto the pan, children will enjoy washing and cutting the fruit, and rolling up the fruit leather.

* ⚹ 2 cups pureed fresh or canned fruit, such as peaches, pears, and strawberries
* ⚹ 1 1/2 teaspoons lemon juice

1. Puree the fruit (no need to peel first) using a food processor or blender. Add lemon juice and mix.
2. Turn a cookie sheet upside-down and stretch plastic wrap over the bottom. Secure the edges with tape.
3. Pour the fruit puree onto the plastic wrap, spreading as evenly as possible. The layer should be about 1/4-inch thick.
4. Bake at 150°F for two to three hours with the oven door slightly ajar (supervise children closely for safety). Remove when the puree is leathery (but not sticky or crispy) to the touch.
5. Cool 10 minutes. Use a pizza cutter to cut the leather into strips. Let children roll up the strips! Makes 10 fruit roll-ups.

Take a Hike!

If possible, take children on an excursion to a nearby park or a wildlife sanctuary with easy hiking trails. If you want to stay closer to home, you can "hike" around your neighborhood. Encourage children to use their imaginations—their neighborhood hike might take them to the Rocky Mountains or Timbuktu!

If you like, you can hike to a special outdoor spot to eat lunch. Let children carry their own lunches in small backpacks and let them take turns being the leader, using the compass or carrying the map. As you walk, remember to stop often to look, listen, and smell. If you happen to see any poison ivy on your trip, point it out and share a bit of hiker's wisdom with children: *Leaves of three, let them be.* When you reach your destination, stop, take a rest, and enjoy lunchtime in the great outdoors!

Book Nook

Even if you're not in the middle of the woods or camping by a babbling brook, these books will make you feel as if you are!

Bailey Goes Camping by Kevin Henkes (Greenwillow, 1985)

Bullfrog and Gertrude Go Camping by Rosamond Dauer (Greenwillow, 1980)

Sally Goes to the Mountains by Stephen Huneck (Abrams, 2001)

Stella and Roy Go Camping by Ashley Wolff (Dutton, 1999)

Three Days on a River in a Red Canoe by Vera B. Williams (Greenwillow, 1984)

Toasting Marshmallows: Camping Poems by Kristine O'Connell George (Clarion, 2001)

Lace a Tent

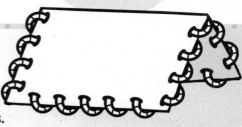

Invite children to lace up their own miniature tents.

Cut a rectangle from lightweight cardboard for each child and punch holes around the edges. Then fold the rectangles in half, creating tent shapes. Let children lace the edges of their tents with yarn. To make lacing easier for children, wrap one end of the yarn with a piece of masking tape. Children might add their tents to the block center to play with later.

Recipe

Goop Soup

In a large dish tub or water table, mix together:

* ✳ one-pound box of cornstarch
* ✳ 1 1/2 cups water
* ✳ food coloring

Provide children with ladles, strainers, plastic bowls, and plastic knives and spoons to explore the material. Add pebbles, pinecones, and twigs for an outdoorsy Goop Soup!

Recipe

No-Fire S'mores

S'mores are the perfect snack to enjoy around the campfire. Have children press a few chocolate chips into large marshmallows (about four or five chips each). Then make sandwich cookies by layering one marshmallow between two graham crackers. Microwave for about 10 seconds, until the marshmallow softens and the chips begin to melt. Press flat, cool slightly, and serve.

Taking Care of Earth

As you hike, picnic, and set up camp this week, teach children the importance of leaving the great outdoors exactly as they found it. Teach children to throw away garbage in garbage cans and to show respect for plants by refraining from picking leaves and flowers or breaking branches. With these earth-friendly habits, children will always have a beautiful camp site to return to, even if it's their own backyard.

Nighttime Nap

The sun may be high in the sky, but with a good imagination, nighttime can be anytime! So why not take a nap "under the stars" today?

Use towels, mats or small blanket for sleeping bags! Choose a "campsite" in your backyard or schoolyard. You can even set up a tent or make one by suspending a sheet (not a blanket) between two clotheslines or tall chairs.

Make a pretend fire by laying rocks in a circle and gathering dry leaves, some kindling, and a log or two. Tell stories around the "campfire." You might even have a snack and sing your favorite campfire songs. Then settle in for a nice, long rest in the great outdoors.

Sand, Sand, Sand!

Children have a natural interest in earthy elements like sand, water, dirt, and mud, and enjoy experimenting with them. A simple material like sand can hold young children's interest for hours as they play, mix, build, and sift. Sand play holds limitless creative potential!

Sand Painting

Children can paint with sand!

Each child will need a heavy sheet of paper or cardboard (cut the top edge into a curvy pattern to represent the water's edge). Set out colored sand (available at craft supply stores, or make your own by adding two tablespoons of powdered tempera paint to one cup of clean sand). Have children paint their paper with thick glue and then sprinkle on different colors of sand to make designs.

Sand Table Fun

Add a new dimension to your sandbox, sand table, water table, or other large container by filling it with clean sand and adding a packet or two of glitter or metallic confetti. Before children arrive, bury seashells and "treasure" such as play coins and costume jewelry in the sand. Then give children buckets to hold their treasures, and then let the hunt begin!

When children have found all the seashells, let them take turns burying their treasures for each other to find. Moistening the sand will create a different medium for children to dig through, and is also great for castle-building and writing in with sticks. For teeny-tiny castles, let children use ice-cube trays!

Sandy Paint

Kids love this textured paint!

Mix together three parts tempera paint with two parts sand. Children can spread their sandy paint on cardboard or heavy paper using thick paint brushes, tongue depressors, or plastic knives. If you live near a beach, invite children to gather shells, seaweed, or beach grass to press into their paintings.

Sand Play Dough

Make a batch of this sandy dough and set out play dough tools along with beach-related cookie cutters (fish, shell, umbrella, sun, and so on). Place children's finished sculptures in the sun to dry. In a few days they will look like sparkling stone!

* 2 cups sand
* 3 tablespoons silver or gold glitter
* 1 cup cornstarch
* 2 teaspoons alum (available in drugstores)
* 1 1/2 cups hot water
* food coloring (optional)

1. Mix sand, glitter, cornstarch, and alum together.
2. Add hot water and stir vigorously (supervise children closely for safety). Add food coloring if desired.
3. Cook the mixture over low to medium heat for about five minutes, until thick. Let cool. Makes three cups.

A Piece of the Beach

Make beautiful beach mementos.

1. To make sand castings, you will need a Styrofoam produce tray for each child, plaster of paris, and an assortment of beach finds, such as shells, seaweed, driftwood, and pebbles.

2. Moisten the sand slightly and have children pat a half-inch layer of sand into each tray. Then have children press their choice of beach treasures lightly into the sand, with their favorite side of each treasure face down. Mix the plaster of paris according to the package directions and pour it carefully over the sand and beach treasures in each tray.

3. To turn the piece of the beach into a wall hanging, cut a loop from a plastic six-pack holder. Press the loop into the plaster at the top of the sand casting before it dries, leaving a portion hanging over the edge to serve as a hanger. Before the plaster is completely set, record the date and the child's name in each casting with a toothpick.

4. When dry, invert the castings, brush off excess sand, and display for a reminder of the beach all year long!

At the Seashore

✳ Talk with children about sand. *What is sand? Where does it come from? How is it made? What plants and animals live in the sand?* (See "All About Sand" below)

✳ Ask for beach-treasure donations. Invite family members and friends to comb the beaches or visit a nature center for shells, pebbles, sand dollars, dried sea grass, driftwood, and other treasures from the seashore for children to explore.

✳ Give children magnifying glasses and invite them to take a close look at grains of sand, rocks, and seashells.

✳ Start a sand collection in labeled baby-food jars. Ask children to bring a sample from any beaches they visit throughout the year. Point out the variety of colors and textures.

Book Nook

Whether at the shore or in your reading nook, a beach umbrella makes a cozy reading spot.

Beach Day by Karen Roosa (Clarion, 2001)

Beach Feet by Lynn Reiser (Greenwillow, 1996)

Sally Goes to the Beach by Stephen Huneck (Abrams, 2000)

Sand in My Shoes by Wendy Kessleman (Hyperion, 1995)

Sand, Sea, Me! by Patricia Hubbell (HarperCollins, 2001)

The Seashore: A First Discovery Book by Gallimard Jeunesse (Scholastic, 1995)

Those Summers by Aliki (HarperCollins, 1996)

Until I Saw the Sea: A Collection of Seashore Poems by Alison Shaw (Holt, 1995)

All About Sand

✳ Sand is a type of soil. Basically, it consists of tiny pieces of rocks or minerals. Most grains of sand were once parts of solid rocks that have crumbled from the crashing of waves.

✳ You can find sand at the bottom of the sea and in many lakes. Sand can wash up from sea bottoms onto beaches, and wind can pile up sand in low hills called sand dunes.

✳ Sand is the color of the mineral from which it is made. In Hawaii you can find black sand, which is made of rocks formed from the hardened lava of volcanoes.

✳ Tiny creatures such as crabs live in sand, artists make sculptures from sand, and geologists study sand!

Fishy Fun!

When children have the opportunity to observe living creatures, they can formulate their own questions and begin to find their own answers. You can give children this opportunity on a daily basis by making a home for a fish in your classroom. All you need are a large glass bowl or small aquarium, a goldfish or two, and some fish food. Children will watch the fish with fascination, enjoy the hands-on feeding sessions, and have lots of fun imitating the movements of their new fishy friends! Give fish plenty of swimming room and a rotating assortment of toys, such as a castle for them to dart through.

1, 2, 3, 4, 5

Use this old favorite to teach the numbers one to ten, the letter Ff and also the concept of left and right.

1, 2, 3, 4, 5
Once I caught a fish alive

6, 7, 8, 9, 10
Then I let it go again

Why did you let it go?
Because it bit my finger so!

Which finger did it bite?
This little finger on the right!

Swimmy Snack

Read aloud *Swimmy* by Leo Lionni (Pantheon, 1963). For snack, give each child a large handful of goldfish crackers and one goldfish-shaped pretzel and invite them to create fish shapes from them, using the pretzel as the eye.

Floating Fish

After reading several books with fishy themes (right), let children create their own fish—and their own fish tales!

1. Blow up balloons halfway and give one to each child. Have children decorate their "fish" with waterproof markers. Then fill a water table or large basin with water, let children put on plastic smocks or bathing suits, and toss in the floating fish.

2. Encourage children to tell a story about their fish, either individually or as a group. Children can pretend to be fish themselves as they tell their stories in the first person. If they need help getting started, ask questions such as: *What kind of fish are you? Are you big or little? What is your name? Where are you swimming?*

3. Record children's stories as they narrate. Then post the stories for family members to read at pick-up time!

Dive into a good book!

Big Al by Andrew Clements (Picture Book Studio, 1988)

Fish Eyes by Lois Ehlert (Harcourt, 1990)

Fish Is Fish by Leo Lionni (Knopf, 1987)

Fish Story by Katherine Andres (Simon & Schuster, 1993)

Louis the Fish by Arthur Yorinks (Farrar Straus & Giroux, 1980)

Rainbow Fish by Marcus Pfister (North South Books, 1992)

Tip
Write each child's name or initials on the back of each piece to avoid a "fish scramble." Store each fish puzzle in a separate plastic self-sealing bag.

Fish Puzzles

Cut simple fish shapes out of posterboard or lightweight cardboard. Have children paint their fish with watercolors. When dry, draw wavy lines on each fish to divide it into three to eight pieces. (Use fewer pieces to make it easier and more to make it harder.) Then cut along the lines to create puzzle pieces. Invite children to mix up their puzzle pieces and put their fish back together again.

Let's Go Fishing

Invite children to go fishing indoors!

1. Cut out several paper fish and let children use markers to color them on one side. On the reverse side of each fish, write a simple activity, such as *touch your toes three times, hop on one foot across the room,* or *do a crab walk twice around the fish pond.*

2. Slip a metal paper clip onto each fish's "nose," then place fish in a "pond" such as a small plastic tub, a hula-hoop, or even blocks arranged in a circle. Use wrapping paper or paper towel tubes to make fishing poles. Tape one end of a string to the tube and tie a magnet to the other end.

3. Invite children to go fishing! They can take turns catching a fish and acting out the activity on the back. When children have caught all the fish, toss them back in the pond!

Fishy Friends

Pet fish are inexpensive and easy to care for. Whether you have two goldfish in a bowl or a school of colorful fish in a tank complete with filter, aerator, and plants, children will be fascinated by your new pets. Let children name their fish and work together to feed and care for them. (Remember that goldfish need just a pinch of food once a day.) Children will expand on their understanding of animals as they learn responsibility and cooperation.

The Ocean Deep

Have children paint a large piece of white butcher paper with blue and green watercolors or fingerpaint. Use as a background for a bulletin board!

Feed the Fish

Take children on a walk to a neighborhood pond and bring along a bag of stale bread or crackers. Let children toss in the crumbs to try to attract hungry fish. As children observe the fish, ask questions such as: *How do fish breathe? How do they use their fins and tails to move?* Or, simply watch your pet fish swim in the bowl!

Notes